"In telling the story of Sammy Younge, Forman has recorded what I suspect will become a classic case history of . . . the radicalization of middle-class black youth . . . . Without a thought to art, with only a desire to tell the world just who Sammy Younge was, he has produced a story with the punch of a novel. . . ."
— Julian Bond, *Life*

". . . a passionate indictment of the white racism that killed black student Sammy Younge. . . . A hard and affecting story."
— *Library Journal*

". . . Sammy Younge, a student at Tuskegee, was shot down in a gas station in 1965 after refusing to use the black toilet. . . . He had learned the lesson which Mr. Forman . . . emphasizes throughout — that to live as a black man in white America you have to be ready to die. . . . To be read, as designated, both as a memorial and as a manifesto."
—*Virginia Kirkus Service*

"An important, troubling book. . . . The author interviewed everyone who knew Younge, and their verbatim conversations describe not one youth but a seething segment of an entire population."
— *Publishers' Weekly*

Sammy Younge, Jr.

Sammy Younge, Jr.

The first Black college student to die in the
Black Liberation Movement

by James Forman

Open Hand Publishing Inc.
Washington, D.C.

Copyright © 1986 by James Forman

Open Hand Publishing Inc.
210 Seventh Street, S.E., Suite A24
Washington, D.C. 20003
Phone (202) 659-9250

Library of Congress
Library of Congress Cataloging-in-Publication Data

Forman, James, 1928-
    Sammy Younge, Jr.: The first black college student to die in the black liberation movement.

        Reprint. Originally published: New York: Grove Press, 1968.
        Includes index.
        1. Younge, Sammy, 1944-1966.   2. Afro-American
students — Alabama — Tuskegee — Biography.   3. United
States — Race relations.   4. Afro-Americans — Civil
rights.   I. Title.
E185.97.Y64F6   1986   973'.00496073'0924 [B] 85-32095
ISBN 0-940880-12-1
ISBN 0-940880-13-X (pbk.)

First published in 1968 by
Grove Press, Inc., New York

Printed in the United States of America
91   90   89   88   87   86   7   6   5   4   3   2   1

To

Huey P. Newton
Charles Koen
H. Rap Brown
— and all the others who will

Take

Care of

Business

Author's Note

The author wishes to thank all those family members, friends, and acquaintances of Sammy Younge for the information and understanding they provided. The cooperation of those persons listed as personages was essential and indispensable. I should also like to thank all those who formed the Committee to Publish Sammy Younge; an unofficial committee that transcribed tapes, typed and read, reread, discussed, edited, and consequently assisted in the publication of this book. It was our mandate that this book should stand as a living memorial to our slain brother, Sammy Younge, Jr. Those of us who knew him cannot forget this fact. The author, therefore, knows that this book belongs to humanity in general and to the Black Liberation struggle in particular. My role was to document a period in history, the life of Sammy Younge, so that his contemporaries—other black students, those in the current Black Liberation struggle, and those who will follow—do not forget that the seeds of liberation are watered with the blood of martyrs.

Contents

Lists of Personages

(in alphabetical order)

Norman "Duke" Barnett: Native of Alabama and a Tuskegee community organizer, known for his fearlessness and ability to defend himself with a shotgun.

Eldridge Burns: Childhood friend of Sammy Younge; the two families were very close.

Stokely Carmichael: Movement activist since 1961; helped develop the "Black Panther Party" in Lowndes County in 1965–66, a project in which Tuskegee students, including Sammy Younge, often participated; Chairman of the Student Nonviolent Coordinating Committee (SNCC), 1966–67.

Mary Ellen Gale: Reporter for *The Southern Courier*.

Edith Gordon: Student at Tuskegee Institute and acquaintance of Sammy Younge.

Bill "Winky" Hall: SNCC campus organizer at Tuskegee 1965–66; SNCC field secretary in Harlem 1966–68.

Jennifer Lawson: Tuskegee student who left school following Sammy Younge's death to become a full-time SNCC worker; an artist active in developing educational materials for the Lowndes County movement and many SNCC projects.

Marilyn "Maggie" Magee: Sammy Younge's English

11

("Communications") teacher at Tuskegee Institute; participated in faculty and student activity.

Fred Meely: SNCC worker active in 1965 demonstrations in Montgomery, later director of SNCC office in Montgomery; subsequently based at Philadelphia and New York offices of SNCC.

Doris Mitchell: Tuskegee resident who knew Sammy from childhood; teacher and veterinarian; promoted relations between Africa and Afro-Americans for mutual support and economic development.

Kathleen Neal: Tuskegee resident, she also spent some of her early years in Asia and Africa where her father served in the U.S. diplomatic corps; later a SNCC worker; married Eldridge Cleaver, minister of information of the Black Panther Party, and became herself communications secretary of that Party.

Wendell "Wendy" Paris: Childhood friend of Sammy Younge and student activist who often worked closely with Sammy.

Gwen Patton: Originally from Detroit, became student activist at Tuskegee; president of Student Government 1965–66; later very active in national anti-war movement.

Laura Payton: Student at Tuskegee Institute.

William Porter: SNCC worker since 1961; one of the directors of the 1965 Washington Lobby in which Sammy Younge participated; based in Atlanta national office of SNCC.

Ann Pratt: Student at Tuskegee Institute.

Willie Ricks: One of SNCC's main Southern field organizers since 1963; active in Birmingham demonstrations and many others; the first SNCC worker to enunciate the cry for Black Power, in 1966.

Demetrius "Red" Robinson: Tuskegee Institute student.

Jimmy Rogers: Student at Tuskegee and staff worker for SNCC in Alabama; witnessed the 1965 murder of Jonathan Daniels in Lowndes County and the finding of Sammy Younge's body in 1966.

Arthur Scavella: Mathematics instructor at Tuskegee Institute who ran for the Board of Education in the 1966 Democratic primary.

Simuel Schutz: A close friend and associate of Sammy Younge; sentenced in 1966 to three years of prison for being one day late in reporting to his draft board; sentenced in 1967 to five years for demonstrating at the Atlanta induction center.

Scott B. Smith: Formerly active in Chicago CORE, joined SNCC and became main organizer in Barbour County (the home of George Wallace); militant student leader at Tuskegee Institute.

Ernest Stephens: Native of Tuskegee, active in SNCC's campus program since 1966; editor of *Black Thesis* (Tuskegee student publication).

Ruby Taylor: Student at Tuskegee and a civil-rights worker in the adjoining rural areas.

George Ware: President of Student Government at Tuskegee Institute 1964–65; active in Montgomery demonstrations; obtained his M.A. and became a full-time SNCC worker in 1966; delegate to Organization of Latin American Solidarity (OLAS) in Havana, 1967; elected SNCC deputy chairman in charge of campus programs, 1968.

Laly Washington: Childhood friend of Sammy Younge and daughter of Mrs. Louise Washington; particularly helpful in portraying Sammy's early years.

Mrs. Louise Washington: An old friend of the Younge family and active in Tuskegee political life.

Jean Wiley: Woodrow Wilson scholar, teacher of Communications at Tuskegee Institute 1964–66, active in student movement; her Tuskegee home was a rest haven for many SNCC staffers, and she subsequently worked as communications officer in the New York SNCC office in 1967.

Aufait Williams: Student at Tuskegee Institute.

Michael Wright: Tuskegee student activist working closely with SNCC since 1966; main force behind 1968 drive for campus reforms; expelled and later put on probation for throwing eggs at U.S. State Department representatives visiting Tuskegee.

Mr. and Mrs. Sammy Younge, Sr.:   Parents of Sammy Younge, Jr.

Major Dates in the Life of Samuel Leamon Younge, Jr.

November 17, 1944	Born in Tuskegee, Alabama
September, 1957 to January, 1960	Attended Cornwall Academy, Great Barrington, Massachusetts
May, 1962	Graduated from Tuskegee Institute High School
June 8, 1962 to July 8, 1964	Served in the United States Navy
January, 1965	Entered Tuskegee Institute as a freshman
January 3, 1966	Shot to death in Tuskegee, Alabama

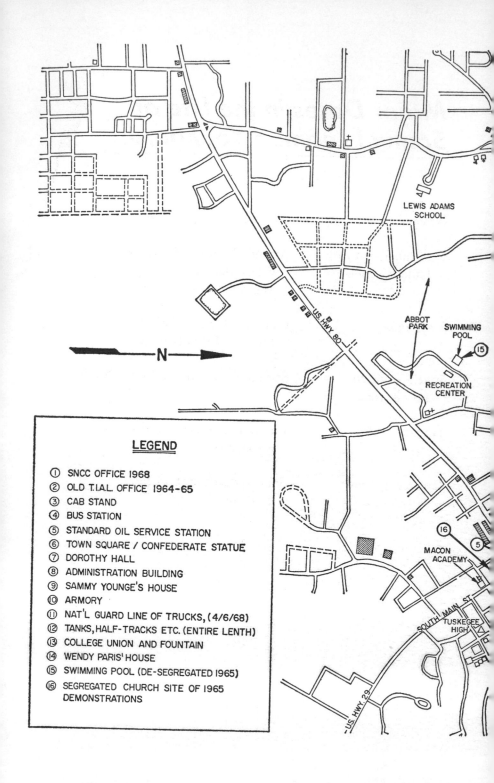

N

LEWIS ADAMS
SCHOOL

US HWY 80

ABBOT
PARK

SWIMMING
POOL
⑮

RECREATION
CENTER

LEGEND

① SNCC OFFICE 1968
② OLD T.I.A.L. OFFICE 1964-65
③ CAB STAND
④ BUS STATION
⑤ STANDARD OIL SERVICE STATION
⑥ TOWN SQUARE / CONFEDERATE STATUE
⑦ DOROTHY HALL
⑧ ADMINISTRATION BUILDING
⑨ SAMMY YOUNGE'S HOUSE
⑩ ARMORY
⑪ NAT'L GUARD LINE OF TRUCKS, (4/6/68)
⑫ TANKS, HALF-TRACKS ETC. (ENTIRE LENTH)
⑬ COLLEGE UNION AND FOUNTAIN
⑭ WENDY PARIS' HOUSE
⑮ SWIMMING POOL (DE-SEGREGATED 1965)
⑯ SEGREGATED CHURCH SITE OF 1965
    DEMONSTRATIONS

⑯
MACON
ACADEMY
⑤

SOUTH MAIN ST.

TUSKEGEE
HIGH

US HWY 29

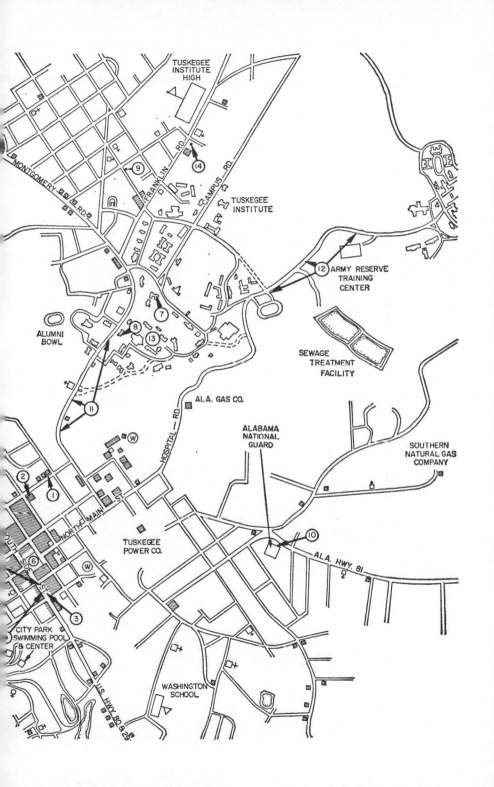

1 *One Funeral Too Many*

This is how it was:

On Tuesday, January 4, 1966, in New York City, I heard the following announcement over WINS, a local radio station:

> Samuel Younge, Junior, a student at Tuskegee Institute, was killed last night at a gas station in Tuskegee, Alabama. Samuel Younge had been active in civil-rights activity in the county. It is reported that he was killed while trying to use a white restroom at the gas station. Civil-rights leaders plan massive demonstrations protesting his killing.

"Did he say 'Sammy Younge'?" I said to myself. I was sure he had, but could that be the Sammy Younge I knew, a friend of mine who was a student at Tuskegee and for whose involvement in the Movement I felt somewhat responsible? I stayed glued to the radio waiting for the next news announcement. He had said "Sammy Younge." I cursed the dirty bastards who had killed him, calling them all sorts of names.

I called the national office of SNCC (Student Nonviolent Coordinating Committee) and learned that the funeral was scheduled for the next day, Wednesday. They were holding a memorial service on the campus of Tuskegee Institute that same day, Tuesday. I could not understand why the memorial and funeral services were being held so quickly. I began to wonder if they wanted to inter the body before a proper examination could be made, or if they felt that by a quick funeral they could subdue what must have been mounting anger among the students.

All during the plane ride to Atlanta that night, I kept

thinking of different people who had been murdered by Southern racists—and how all their killers had gone free. I remembered how Richmond Flowers, the Attorney General of Alabama, had made headlines nationwide by attacking the corrupt jury system of Southern states, a system that made it possible for white people to kill blacks and then be tried by all-white juries, with a select Negro here and there. I kept wondering if, in Tuskegee with its eight per cent black population, Sammy's killer would also go free, even if they caught him. I felt he would. And then I thought of Emmett Till in Money, Mississippi, and Charles Mack Parker, and Chaney, Goodman, and Schwerner, and the unnamed black bodies we were always finding in Mississippi.

"It's a wonder many more haven't been killed," I told myself, attempting to rationalize away, or maybe to state, the truth. The year 1966 was going to be decisive, a turning point. I felt we were not going to remain tactically nonviolent too much longer. Over the years, there had been an erosion of this concept.

In Atlanta, our executive committee was attempting to hold a meeting that Wednesday morning. Some of the members had attended the memorial service and were utterly disgusted by the nature of it; they believed that the school administration was trying to keep the lid on protest and prevent violent retaliation by the student body. That was why the school had its memorial service early, they felt. I concurred.

All that morning, I halfheartedly participated in the meeting, knowing full well that I had to leave soon to attend the funeral. I simply did not want to attend another "civil-rights funeral."

"Okay, let's go, we got two hours to get there," said

Cleve Sellers, then SNCC program secretary. Two years later, he himself would be wounded by the bullets of white racists in Orangeburg, South Carolina.

"Cleve, I just don't want to go. I can't make it," I told him.

"You got to go. They been asking for you. Wondering why you weren't at the memorial service yesterday. I explained that, but not this. Let's go."

"Naw, man . . . I'm just tired of going to funerals for civil-rights people."

"Me too, Jim."

"I guess you're right," I told him. "I got to go." That had been clear all along; it was a matter of facing up to it.

"Let's make it. Stanley Wise is going with us. We'll make it, but you got to move."

As we pulled into Tuskegee, we were dressed in typical SNCC style. Cleve began to put on his starched overalls as we hunted for the church. Stanley changed shirts while driving. I looked at my rather raggedy suit; I thought I had a tie in my pocket, but no.

We parked the car and walked slowly toward the church. The small building was mostly filled with students from Tuskegee Institute. Some people from the community were there, too. We walked down the side aisle, taking seats in the middle of the left-hand section. Directly in front of us were the marshals, friends of ours, many of whom had become involved in the Movement over the past year. Among them was Bill Hall. We had planned to catch the same plane from New York but had missed one another; I wondered how he had got to Tuskegee.

All the male marshals were dressed in black suits and ties with white shirts; the girls were in black dresses. Sammy's coffin was directly in front of the altar, lying open.

People walked up to see his face for the last time. An American flag draped the casket.

After some hestitation, Cleve, Stanley, and myself walked up to the casket and stood by it for a few seconds. I wondered what they were thinking. "That could be you," I said to myself. "It could have been you many times in the past. It may well be you in the future. . . ."

The American flag. Killed in civil-rights combat. The United States of America. Veteran Number. . . . Known. . . . Unknown. Twenty-one years old.

We went back to our seats. The family had entered; there was complete silence. The service began. I kept watching his mother and father. Though I had never met them, I felt very close to them. Mrs. Younge looked like my mother in many ways—thin, olive-colored, hair turning a lovely gray, a face that showed the strength of years behind it. The Tuskegee choir sang "The Battle Hymn of the Republic." They sang it; they really did, that day.

The church waited for the family to file out. They passed near us. It was hard, very hard, to keep back the tears. The sorrow for the family, the anguish, the hate, the desire for vengeance—all surged forth in me. Twenty-one years old. Killed in civil-rights combat. Not the first, not the last. How many more? I tried to stop the train of thought. I tried closing my eyes to freeze the tears, to choke the pain. But it churned on and on and on. How many more? That's all I could think of.

We went outside. I walked away from my friends. I thought of my involvement with Sammy, with the Tuskegee students. Of how crying would not help. If only we were in a shooting war with the crackers. If only we could kill some of *them*. Maybe then having a friend killed would not cause this kind of anguish. We would get some of them if they got some of us. The war ought to be open. But we weren't killing back. We were not in a shooting war. We were at war but they had the guns, they ran the legal machinery. Sammy, just another dead nigger.

I walked to the car, crying as I never cried before. I was unable to stop. Then, I didn't want to stop. I wanted all the pain to come forth. The grief for the family. The fear for the lives of all those working with SNCC who lived on the thin line between life and death every time they rode an Alabama back road or a Mississippi highway. The fear I had put into my own epitaph, which I delivered at the beginning of the Mississippi Summer Project of 1964. It was in Chicago, Illinois, at a rally for some thirty-five thousand people in Soldiers Field—on the same day that Chaney, Goodman, and Schwerner were killed, though we did not know it then:

> If there is one death in Mississippi this summer, all of us—and especially President Lyndon Baines Johnson—must bear responsibility. He has not heard our call for federal protection in Mississippi. We can send black men to Vietnam, but we cannot provide protection in Mississippi. And if I die this summer, take my body and cremate it; divide the ashes in four parts. Throw one fourth on the steps of the United States White House, one fourth on the steps of the United States Justice Department, one fourth in the halls of the Congress of the United States, and one fourth here in Washington Park where I played as a kid.

There have been so many deaths; old people, young people, black people, white people. Hundreds of thousands have gone to jail. Many have been beaten, with permanent damage to their bodies. Some students from Alcorn College disappeared; one unidentified body was later found in the Mississippi River. But Sammy was the first black college student active in the Movement to have been killed. We knew Sammy. We worked with him. He worked with us. We helped to develop him. He helped us.

Sammy is dead. He was a leader in the Tuskegee community. We all die. We suppress thoughts of the one certainty of life: death. The idea that we shall live no more. We must say to other black college students around the country: you live; you will die. Only when we overcome the fear of death—only then—can we really live for the liberation of man.

We drove in the long procession going to the cemetery. Sammy's grave was at the base of a hill. It had been raining hard and the yellow dirt had turned to mud, difficult to walk on. The marshals lowered the casket. The last words were said. The family left. Wendy Paris and Simuel Schutz stood there. They were taking it very hard. They stood in silence, looking at the half-filled space in the ground. Wendy wanted to say something, tried to talk. He picked up a yellow tulip from the flowers lying there. He held it between his large brown hands as a man might offer a rose to the one he loved, about to depart on a long journey. He and Sammy had been close friends, road buddies. Schutz, too. Sammy had become the student leader; now they had to carry on.

Wendy turned to go, paused, turned around again. He let the tulip fall. Shook his head and shoulders in that way of his, but never like this. Wanting, trying to say something. He just lowered his head, shaking it. Then he put his arm around Simuel Schutz. "Sammy's gone, Schutz. He's gone." They walked away, heads down, their arms around each other, holding each other together.

Cleve and I walked up to the grave. He touched his

forehead in a kind of salute. I plucked a few fern leaves, dropped them, and cried the last time for Sammy.

That same day, I decided to write the story of Sammy's life. We in SNCC had a special responsibility to him, I felt— a responsibility which we must carry to other young black students across the country, especially in the Deep South. Telling his story was one way to do this, and I started to work on it immediately. The book had to be more than just a memorial, a tribute. I wanted not only to describe the events in his life but also to discuss and analyze situations in which he had found himself while working for civil rights. I wanted to portray a time in history, a period through which the student protest movement had passed.

In many ways the murder of Sammy Younge marked the end of tactical nonviolence: the long marches where blacks were expected to undergo harsh treatment by white Southern crackers, not protecting themselves, not fighting back—that day was over. When it occurs today, nonviolence is but the lingering edge of a phase in the struggle.

Sammy's murder also marked the end of any hope that the federal government would intervene and protect the rights of black people in this country. Time and again, the government had demonstrated that it would not; Sammy's murder was one too many. There are few, if any, militant blacks today who expect this government to do much for us.

Three days after Sammy's murder, the Student Non-violent Coordinating Committee issued a statement opposing the war in Vietnam. In that statement, we pointed out that the murder of Sammy Younge had taken place at a time when the U.S. government was sending black youths, as well as white youths, to Vietnam to fight for the "free-

dom" of others while, in our own country, many government officials openly avow racism. To many black young
men, Sammy Younge's murder further indicated that their
role was to fight not in Vietnam but here in the United
States, for the freedoms they are denied. Simuel Schutz
feels this way, and within a year of Sammy's death he was
fighting a three-year prison sentence for being one day late
in reporting to his draft board—a segregated draft board in
the same county where Sammy had been killed.

The life and death of Sammy Younge were important
for still other reasons. Sammy was active in the Movement
during a period of intense internal conflicts within and
between civil-rights organizations. The former pleas for
unity, the submerging of basic political differences for the
undefined common cause—all these efforts were unmasked
as Sammy became more and more involved in the Movement. For years, everyone in the civil-rights movement had
known that the alliances of many groups would come to an
end one day. As the chips piled up and the stakes went
higher, the players were less kind, less indulgent. The cry,
"We all want the same thing," became a myth destroyed.

Sammy Younge was active in a period when Democratic and Republican politicians around the country still
held up Macon County as a model for the "New South."
There, in a county where blacks outnumber whites seven
to one, traditional Negro political leaders were urging bi-
racial politics: "We must not seem to be racists in reverse."
They even urged black voters in Macon County to vote for
Bull Conner, the notorious Birmingham Chief of Police
who loosed dogs on black men, women, and children.
"Vote for Bull Conner as the Alabama National Committeeman in the Democratic Party," they said. Throughout
the United States, there are enclaves of middle-class Negroes who feel they are immune to the pressures and acts of

racist white politicians, cops, and hoodlums. The murder of
Sammy Younge shattered this myth for those who would
see. The myth is dying elsewhere, too.

Sammy's murder increased the alienation of many students at Tuskegee and on campuses across the South. It is
my hope that a book about Sammy will further their alienation from the American values of 'make money, live well,
look out for yourself, don't worry about the other guy, get
it while the getting is good, live it up!'

With these ideas in mind, I talked with Sammy's
friends and family about the book. A few days after the
funeral, I began interviewing many of them, individually
and in groups, tape recording our talks. This book, then, is
the story of Sammy's life as told by his parents, friends,
teachers, fellow students, and co-workers from SNCC, with
my own commentary from time to time. It is a book of
many voices, all telling about Sammy and the world in
which he lived. Although each of the speakers is identified,
they are not individually as important as the picture which
emerges: a portrait of the life of one young black man and
his time.

While interviewing people, I was aware that so often
in the Movement we just describe the facts. Someone is in
jail. Others are beaten. One more killed here, two more
there, three over yonder; but the Movement is more than
a set of facts. It is not just people who go around demonstrating. We have love-lives. We have conflicts. We have
vocations, aspirations, personal problems, dreams deferred.
I wanted to go beneath the surface, to reach down and
bring forth all the humanity of Sammy Younge.

Sammy's mother once told me when we were discussing the book, "The only thing that I don't want is something superficial. And it seems to me that so little can be

said about Sammy except maybe his being in this civil-
rights movement, which is all right. But perhaps I'm being
modest. I'm his mother, and maybe I'm injecting myself
into it—injecting my aspirations and my hopes and my desires into what he actually did. I often say to myself, how
can other people see my child in this light—like a hero—
when I hadn't seen him in this light myself? But it wakes
me up. . . ." She showed me a card she had sent to all the
people who had written condolences. Inscribed on it were
some words from Kahlil Gibran's *The Prophet:*

> And a woman who held a babe against
> her bosom said, Speak to us of Children.
>   And he said:
> Your children are not your children.
> They are the sons and daughters of Life's
> longing for itself. . . .
> You may give them your love
> but not your thoughts,
> For they have their own thoughts.
> You may house their bodies
> but not their souls,
> For their souls dwell in the house
> of tomorrow, which you cannot visit,
> not even in your dreams.
> You may strive to be like them,
> but seek not to make them like you.
> For life goes not backward
> nor tarries with yesterday.*

* Copyright 1923 by Kahlil Gibran; renewal copyright 1951 by Administrators C.T.A. of Kahlil Gibran Estate, and Mary G. Gibran. Reprinted
by permission of Alfred A. Knopf, Inc., publishers.

II Roots

Tuskegee, Alabama—the seat of Macon County—is a sleepy town of some seven thousand people, centered around a large, open square in the traditional style of the South. Except for Saturdays, when black folk come from all over Macon and the adjoining counties to shop and to socialize, there are few people on the square. In its center, on a separate rectangle of grass, stands the statue of a Confederate soldier erected in memory of those who fought hard to preserve slavery and to keep the wealth of the South in the South. Around the square are a few stores and the Alabama Exchange Bank: fairly new buildings, functional, of no special character. On one side is the courthouse, a creaky old building with faded, red brick walls. This square represents the center of white power—the bankers, store-owners and lawmen who actually control Macon County and its eighty-five per cent black population.

Those who live in the vicinity of the square are mostly the "town niggers" as opposed to the "Tuskegee Institute niggers," who live not in Tuskegee but in Tuskegee Institute, about five minutes' drive away. The difference is not merely one of names. Tuskegee Institute, Alabama, has its own post office and two important institutions. One of these is the Veterans' Administration Hospital, founded in 1924 to take care of Southern black veterans who found it difficult—sometimes impossible—to get medical treatment in the segregated white hospitals. The other is the college, Tuskegee Institute, for which the township was named. Together they make this small area unique in two ways: as a pocket of black affluence amid the poverty of a typical Black Belt county, and as a center of high educational and

29

professional achievement in a seat of semi-literacy (white as well as black).

Tuskegee Institute was originally founded by Booker T. Washington in 1880 as the Tuskegee State Normal School: a place to train young blacks for agricultural, mechanical, and other non-professional work then considered appropriate to their station in life. It was Washington's belief that "Brains, prosperity, and character for the Negro will settle the question of civil rights. . . . The great thing is for us as a race to conduct ourselves so as to become worthy of the privileges of a United States citizen, and these privileges will come." George Washington Carver continued this tradition in the twentieth century, making the Institute famous through his experiments in its science laboratories to develop hundreds of products utilizing peanuts and sweet potatoes.

Washington's philosophy that blacks should win acceptance by diligence, modest ambition, and non-involvement in politics would have a long-lasting effect on the residents of Tuskegee—as it did on black people across the United States. While the Institute became more academic in name, physical appearance, and curriculum over the years, it did not change much in spirit. Ralph Ellison, a Tuskegee graduate, described the character of the Institute (without naming it as such) in *The Invisible Man:*

> It was a beautiful college. The buildings were old and covered with vines and the roads gracefully winding, lined with hedges. . . . I've recalled it often here in my hole: How the grass turned green in the springtime . . . how the moon shone down on the buildings, how the bell in the chapel tower rang out. . . . Then in my mind's eye I see the bronze statue of the college Founder, the cold Father symbol, his hands outstretched in the breathtaking gesture of lifting a veil that flutters in hard, metallic folds above the face of a kneeling slave;

and I am standing puzzled, unable to decide whether
the veil is really being lifted, or lowered more firmly
in place; whether I am witnessing a revelation or a more
efficient blinding.

In his time, however, few residents shared Ellison's doubts
about that veil.

Today, green grass and trees and pleasant homes
abound in the town of Tuskegee Institute. Neatly clipped
lawns contrast sharply with the shacks and dirt roads of
surrounding Macon County. The families who live here
are mostly attached either to the college or the hospital; it
is clear that they are relatively well-off and stable. Mr. and
Mrs. Samuel Younge, Sr., who head one of these families,
live only a few blocks from the Institute in a modest but
comfortable six-room house which they built after they
married and settled permanently in Tuskegee. Sammy, Jr.,
their son, grew up in that house.

Mr. Younge was often away from home for long
periods, and it was Mrs. Renee Younge who played the
major role in bringing up Sammy. She is a slim, very light-
skinned woman, an elementary-school teacher by profession. I had not met her before Sammy was murdered and
it seemed awkward to ask her too many questions about her
son immediately after the funeral. At our first meeting,
therefore, we talked only of the projected book and a little
about Sammy's childhood. A year later we met again, and
this time I realized that she too had been a freedom fighter,
trying to survive in a society filled with racism and its complex, dehumanizing effects. I became more and more conscious of the various strains in our history as a people. Finally, I realized that there had to be a sub-story in any book
on Sammy: the story of his mother and the sources of her
strength.

MRS. YOUNGE: You could say it was in the family—I mean, the respect that my family had for themselves. Way back when I was a child in Charleston, seven or eight years old, people would call the house and ask for my godfather by his first name. I told them, "You got the wrong number. If you want to speak to *Mr*. Sasportas, that's one thing, but there's nobody here by the name of Sasportas." I said, "Only his friends call him by his first or last name alone." I was raised up like that. Some of my friends were financially deprived, but I've never known them to let their poverty be a deterrent to having pride.

I had a long background of freedom, even though we were often far from affluent. My great-grandmother was a Frenchwoman. The story I heard was that during the French Revolution, this family came with two young girls from the West Indies to Charleston, where they built a large house. One of the girls married and lived in the house. She had twelve children. That was my great-grandmother.

My great-grandfather was half Negro and half Scotch. They tell me that his mother, who was a slave, had been freed by her Scotch husband before he was born, so he was free, too. All the tax records and business records of the house in Charleston list his name and then "F.P.C."—that was a "Free Person of Color." He had twenty-five children, by two wives.

My mother's mother, Isabelle Clyde, was the daughter of an Englishman who owned the Clyde Shipping Line. He hired a tutor for her. She was a very accomplished musician and spoke three or four languages. They all lived in the house in Charleston, which stayed in the family from 1812 to 1939 and became a tourist attraction. The meal was the big thing in our family—like they say, we ate Sunday dinner every day. There was a white tablecloth, silverware, napkin rings and napkins. You sat down and said grace; after dinner, you sat there and talked. If you had fish, you had a certain kind of wine. And if anybody came to visit, that's how we would entertain them.

We had nothing but white neighbors all our lives. Even into my early adult life, Charleston was not strictly zoned because so much property was owned by Negroes from so far back and Charleston had so many of what they called Free Persons of Color. Until after Reconstruction, there were bans on whites marrying slaves in Charleston but not on marrying F.P.C. Also, you couldn't tell a French or Portuguese person not to marry—they weren't citizens.

You could find the same situation in any old seaport town of the South. I knew a white man who lived with a colored woman all his life, in a big house where she had everything she wanted. When he died, he left everything to her. Friends of the man tried to break the will but couldn't. I remember two distant relatives of mine, who were full brothers—one fair and one dark. When their mother died, one of them went to live with a white family and the other with a colored family. They were full brothers but one grew up as white and the other as colored. In Charleston then, the determination of what you were didn't follow a strict race line.

My father was a house painter and my mother was a seamstress. With four children, they had to learn to do things. My father painted all the medallions and the gold things in the Catholic churches. He did some very beautiful and decorative work. He painted houses, too; he could get just the right color blue. Sometimes he mixed his own paint, and if he used paint he had mixed himself, it *stayed*. My mother could make anything she laid eyes on. People who left Charleston and went to New York would ask her to help them when they were fixing up their apartments. Anything that a needle could put together, she could make.

Later, she decided that she could do better financially by going out for day-work. She was proud, determined, smart, hard-working—liberal with us in some ways but not others.

When I was fourteen, I went to live with my god-parents who were also in Charleston. I had spent a lot of time with them anyway: they had no children and wanted me to live with them. They had more to give, but even then I never had money to waste. My godmother said, "You get what you need—not what you want." You couldn't just sit down and say, "I want a new coat," and get one unless you needed it.

My godfather was a handsome man. He had very smooth skin with a lot of red in it. We went to get on the train once, and they tried to send me to the "white" coach and him to the other.

I never ran into disrespect until I left the private Catholic school and went to public school. Kids would say, "Don't play with her, she's a mulatto." At that time, "mulatto" carried the connotation of being a bastard; it meant one of your parents was black and one was white and it was against the law for them to marry. I wish I had a dollar for every fight I was in—it wasn't fighting with friends, it was strictly racial. You know how boys try to make you step off the sidewalk. I'd never get off. I'd wriggle around somewhere. I didn't have any fear. I obviously thought I was starting a Negro revolution. And my godfather would always tell me, "I won't live to see it, but you may. And your children will live to see it—see the darker races of the world rise up and claim their place in society."

I went on to Knoxville College, where there was this teacher from Pittsburgh who had read about the South and the Negro. She and I used to get into it all the time. At the end of the summer, my parents received a letter saying that I had been a big disappointment, etc.— I can almost remember every word of it—and that when I came back to school, I would be on probation. You can imagine what kind of day that was in my house. They said, "Hey, are you dumb to have deserved a letter like this!" They acted like I was a campus fighter, but this wasn't so. I hadn't done anything to deserve a letter like that.

The next morning my father put me on a bus and took me to Knoxville and stood me up in front of the president and said, "Here she is, what has she done? What has she done to deserve a letter like this? When you write a letter like this, you have to have charges. You have to have something concrete." The president said, "I have to check with the dean." So he checked with the dean, and the dean squirmed around. Then he checked with the house mother, and the house mother squirmed around. That's how I happened to go back to Knoxville College. I went there for two years and then to Spelman in Atlanta. After I graduated, I went to Talladega to teach.

At Talladega, Sammy's mother met the man she would later marry. Samuel Younge, Sr.—tall, heavy-set, somewhat darker in color than his wife—came from a Tuskegee family which included some well-to-do, professional Negroes. During Sammy's lifetime, Mr. Younge was an occupational therapist and became head of the Department of Physical Medicine and Rehabilitation at the Veterans' Hospital; later he joined the U.S. Forest Service in Atlanta, Georgia. Although he seemed to be less aggressive on the issue of racism than his wife, Mr. Younge also had an independent spirit.

MR. YOUNGE: Tuskegee is my family's home. I have a huge family here, some thirty people right now. My grandparents were slaves. My grandfather was here before

Tuskegee Institute was built. Somewhere around the establishment of that institution, he built the red house you see out that window. I own the property right through here.

There was a different philosophy in those days—Booker T. Washington's influence was here. He became an idol, I guess, to the whites. Things just moved along, in a separate pattern. I always called Tuskegee the Nigger Air Base because that's about what it was.* There were people like W.E.B. DuBois who didn't like Booker Washington's "separate but equal" approach, but the Southern whites liked it. When he went over to the Atlanta Exposition in 1898 and started associating with Jay Gould and the Rockefellers, he had it made. Old Booker, he was pretty astute. His philosophy fitted that era; it wouldn't fit now. It wouldn't work now. It didn't work much in that era, either —just in some instances.

My father was born here, then migrated to Birmingham and then to Pittsburgh. I came back here to go to school. After that, I'd leave to work and then I would come back and work and then I'd leave to work, come back. See, I have a philosophy—don't stay on a job over five years.

I went to college at Talladega for four years. I graduated in 1928. I think the catalogue said that we were supposed to read a whole series of books. Did I read them? No. Words like "the invisible man"—I've heard them, but I've never read that book. The man who wrote that book went to Tuskegee and he came back here. I went up to hear him speak and to get the word. So I can talk a little about literary things, by osmosis.

I read *Gone With the Wind*, but I don't know why. I think I was in that CCC [Civilian Conservation Corps]

---

* During World War II, Tuskegee became the site of the first training base for black pilots; this establishment later closed down.

camp out in the woods, twelve or fifteen miles back of Northport, Alabama. There was a race riot there, on Valentine's Day—at night, really—back in 1934. It all started on the right to have a coffee break or a smoke break. There was a direct order from the War Department that there was to be a smoke break—five or ten minutes. It was an all-Negro camp, with white foremen. The whites resented that right to smoke. It led to a little head-knocking. A Negro was arguing with a white foreman out in the woods. The white man swung at the Negro but missed him. The Negro backs off and grabs a large rock and conks the man. The feeling is getting higher. The six or eight white foremen begin to get on the telephone to contact the Klan.

Then it ballooned up at supper. The lieutenant went in the mess hall and the pie-throwing started. The pumpkin pies were just ruining this lieutenant. The Negroes broke into the warehouse and got picks and shovels. The sheriff was ordered to come to arrest the Negro boy who had been leading some of this business, and he brings the Klan with him. They arrested the boy. The Negroes saw him handcuffed and in the car. They grabbed their shovels and rushed the car. Then the Ku Klux rushed them. They had teenagers with them. I remember one who was about twelve years old, and he had a rifle. I said to myself, "This is really training them." It didn't last long. The next day, the Army discharged eighty of the Negroes.

I wasn't involved—I was working in the office. Before that, I had been teaching school in Tuscaloosa [Alabama] and somebody said, "The CCC people want a typist." I couldn't type, so I rented a machine and pecked out a letter of application. I went out to that camp and this West Point lieutenant said, "Boy, you type?" I said, "Yes, sir." He had me type out something and hired me on the spot. That was thirty dollars a month plus room and board. Before, I had been making just thirty dollars. I didn't have much to do—that's the reason I read *Gone With the Wind*. And I could smoke any time.

I wasn't too race-conscious at that time. The first time I realized color was a factor was one time when I tried to get a Pullman. We don't have any race consciousness sitting here in our house in Tuskegee. We're isolated.

A close friend of the Younge family, Mrs. Louise Washington, explained this isolation and how it had been sustained over the years.

MRS. WASHINGTON: Most of the better things here are for Negroes rather than whites. We didn't feel deprived; it was only when you left the community that it hit you. We felt that our schools, especially the elementary schools, were superior to the ones that the whites had. All of the fine entertainments came out here. There was no symphony, no library, nothing of any value in town. We had the better swimming pool. You never had any discourtesy; you never had any meanness. Some of the rural people did, but we were unaware of this. The whites would "Mrs." you just as courteous and nice when you'd go downtown. So the children, as they grew up in this community, were usually six or seven years old before they even knew that there was such a thing as a Negro and a white man. They didn't have to come in contact with this. They knew that they were Negroes, of course, but not what it actually meant.

I registered to vote as soon as I was twenty-one with no difficulty. At that time, I had some political interest and awareness and I was very upset because everybody wouldn't go down and register. There was no interest, no mass interest. Shortly after, around '46 or '48, when this interest did come about, then they tightened. There was no impoliteness or overt discourtesy—it just took you three hours to fill out the forms. Of course people become discouraged, and that's what they intended.

Some of our people—and Dean Gomillion [Dr. G. C. Gomillion] was one of them—never, never let up. He was constantly trying to organize, trying to get people down to register. We would give two weeks of our time and then he wouldn't hear from us until some cop hit a colored boy out on the highway and then we'd get incensed and we'd follow him again for two or three weeks. He was the only person in this community who kept up the pressure consistently.

Gomillion was the son of an illiterate farm laborer in South Carolina; he had risen to become a sociologist and chairman of Tuskegee Institute's Division of Social Sciences. His efforts to win the vote proved successful despite all the barriers raised: the disqualification of black Ph.D.'s on technicalities, the irregularity and secrecy with which the Boards of Registrars met, the tedious procedures. Before World War II, less than a hundred black people had been registered in Macon County; by 1954, their number was approaching that of the white voters. That year, for the first time since Reconstruction, a Negro (Mrs. Jessie Guzman) ran for office (a seat on the County School Board). She lost, but the very fact of her candidacy—plus the 1954 Supreme Court decision and the Montgomery bus boycott—made the whites nervous. Soon afterward, blacks came to form the majority of registered voters in Tuskegee. Most of them, naturally, were from the Tuskegee Institute middle class.

In 1957, the whites moved to counteract this growth of potential power. The Alabama State Legislature redrew the boundaries of the town to make a twenty-eight-sided figure which excluded Tuskegee Institute—thus keeping all but a few of the registered Negroes from voting in municipal elections.

MRS. WASHINGTON: When the gerrymander came, there was a mass meeting. It was the most emotional experience I've ever had in my life. It just seemed to finally have awakened the people in the community. Dean Gomillion had tried in the past to organize "little trade with your friends," meaning trade with Negroes. We'd trade with our friends for about a month, and then it would sort of disintegrate. The new boycott to fight the gerrymander was the first time he really had massive and prolonged support. (We couldn't call it a boycott, of course, that was illegal. It had to be "selective buying.") I was even able to get my daughter Laly to cooperate with staying out of that dime store during the boycott, and this was not easy. I think the Younges did the same thing. I don't know how the children felt—probably it just meant they couldn't get bubble gum.

This is also when the community really became aware of the TCA. It had started off as a men's civic club, thirty or more years ago. When it became a community thing they changed the name to Tuskegee Civic Association. That was in 1941, I think. So it's a very old Negro organization, but it was during the gerrymander that the community first accepted it as a group that could unite people behind it. Dean Gomillion became head of TCA.

I dare say that our boycott wouldn't have been successful if it were not for the bus boycott in Montgomery. This was one of the rallying cries—"Aren't we going to do what the people in Montgomery did? Are we going to be less proud than the people in Montgomery?" Those people really suffered, but up here we were just inconvenienced. We had cars; we could go to Montgomery and buy groceries. Quite a few of us here went to Montgomery periodically and took turns just picking up people on the street and driving them places. I can remember that President Foster [Dr. Luther Foster of Tuskegee Institute], on the day they announced in Montgomery that everybody would walk whether they had a car or not, had an appointment with the Governor. He walked to the Governor's mansion. When he went in, he said, "I apologize for being late but, you know, we are walking today." I thought this was significant because Dr. Foster didn't have to do that and he did not publicize it.

During the boycott, local business receipts were reportedly cut as much as seventy per cent and some twenty firms closed down. The gerrymander went to the Supreme Court, as the case of *Gomillion v. Lightfoot* (Mayor Lightfoot of Tuskegee), and was defeated by means of a Supreme Court decision of November, 1960. Then, after having fought to keep their voting majority, and won, the blacks of Tuskegee turned around and delivered power back into the hands of the whites. Gomillion, who had once criticized the apolitical philosophy of Booker T. Washington, now maintained that "we didn't wish to control, merely to share." Whites must not be frightened into moving out, the TCA leadership maintained. What TCA did not say was the truth that exists all over this country: the whites are afraid that if we come into power, we will do the same things to them that they have done to us.

In the first election where black voters had a majority, a Negro professor with a Ph.D. sought to run for mayor—

but TCA supported a white man with a seventh-grade education. TCA combined with "white moderates" to elect a City Council composed of two Negroes and four whites.

With that vote, Tuskegee acquired its name as a "model town." The spirit of legalism and conciliation prevailed despite the sit-in movement which erupted in the South in 1960. The social structure of Tuskegee kept it a backwater even during that peak period of black student militancy.

MRS. WASHINGTON: When the Movement started in 1960, the students here wanted very much to become involved. They really wanted to do something. But there wasn't anything here that they felt needed to be attacked. They were so frustrated. Finally they just marched, for two or three days, for no reason except maybe in sympathy for the students who were sitting-in in North Carolina. Dr. Foster led the march downtown. They did this for several days until they felt that they had expressed themselves.

In 1963, right after those children were killed in the Birmingham church, Dr. Foster called a meeting of all the faculty and staff of Tuskegee Institute. Everybody was just so upset. As a matter of fact, two of those children were children of Tuskegee graduates. He called the meeting to see what type of expression or protest was appropriate for the academic community. One of the suggestions was that the faculty should have a protest march. Of course, they didn't do that. People felt it would be a rather futile gesture. People also felt that for a faculty, marching would not be an appropriate type of protest—for students, perhaps, but not for faculty.

This was the world into which Sammy would be born and grow up. To some of his contemporaries, it was far from "model." Three of them—Ernest Stephens, Kathleen Neal Cleaver, and George Ware—gave their views of Tuskegee's history and society.

ERNEST STEPHENS: Students at Tuskegee Institute are told that they must learn to project the Tuskegee image—a very dignified, refined type thing. I remember the orientation for veterinary students. The dean's whole idea was that any black veterinarian who comes out of Tuskegee Institute has to be better than a white student coming out of a white university. He wants to be able to say, "Here stands a veterinarian" and not, "Here stands a veterinarian from a black school." In other words, we must show the white world that we are human, that we are educated and cultured in the same way as they are.

Tuskegee isn't a unique community and the campus situation isn't unique either. It highlights almost every black Southern college. I was in high school, I guess, when I first began to notice that Tuskegee typifies a certain concept: carry on your life in a quiet, dignified manner, gain the respect of the white people who are in control of the town, and thereby further your particular cause. If the problem arises of white people messing over the black community of Tuskegee, you must act on this in a dignified manner. It's a strange thing. You have here a black community which seeks to perpetrate the idea of identifying with the black community. But the way they do this is to show white people that "we" can be separate and yet just as good as you are, by being the same way that you are. That's the whole concept, and everything in Tuskegee is based upon it.

There always has been a tone of pride in that Negroes have had their own homes, their own property, their own businesses. The fight for the vote shook them up. People like Gomillion—a lot of these folks with their Ph.D.'s— went down to register and they ran smack-dab into the Man. They would keep going back and reapplying in a quiet, dignified way; the Man would just take their applications and tear them up. Finally the white folks settled that whole question by cutting all the Negroes out of town with the gerrymander. That really woke people up. Because the white folks essentially said, "These niggers ain't voting." All the time, the intelligentsia in Tuskegee had had the impression that white people regarded them as different from the black folks who worked on farms and so forth. The white folks showed them that there was no difference.

KATHLEEN NEAL: I lived in Tuskegee from age three to nine, and didn't really know what it was all about until I came back here and got involved with SNCC. As a child, I went to an elementary school called Children's House; that was about 1950. The children associated only with each other. You didn't know anything about the people who lived out in the county. Most of the children were light-skinned, because that's what the upper class of Tuskegee is all about. There happened to be one girl in my first-grade class who was black. Now, when the children went outside they were supposed to line up to march. Nobody in the class wanted to line up with her. The teacher asked for volunteers, and I volunteered because I didn't understand. I didn't understand that whole thing.

In the high school you find the same caste distinctions. If your kid hasn't gone to a white liberal prep school in Massachusetts for a year or two, then you're just nowhere. Middle-class people from the Institute or the hospital don't associate with the poor Negroes except when the poor people are their maids and housekeepers and children-keepers. The middle-class group in Tuskegee has a very, very paternalistic attitude toward the non-middle-class group who work in their homes. The whole thing is a parody of white society.

My father's attitude was representative. He thought that Tuskegee was an ideal community in which to bring up a child. He said that he wanted a place where children could live in a normal way—play any place, associate with anybody, and have certain types of advantages. He wanted his children to grow up knowing nothing about racial prejudice, having no racial or class consciousness. This is what he envisioned as normal, good, and ideal. I was never exposed to any kind of discrimination or prejudices. It was a fairy tale.

The majority of the kids I grew up with became very neurotic because they were brought up in this sick, unreal community. They can't do anything, don't want to do anything, except waste money and carouse. Everything was so soft for them. They all had cars or their parents' cars, record players, clothes, and plenty of money.

GEORGE WARE: They go to the so-called best prep schools in the country, and then some of the best colleges in the country. And they become some of the most unproductive people. I could name person after person in Tuskegee who grew up in that atmosphere and who is almost paralyzed in terms of being able to function professionally, socially, and otherwise. Some of the most talented people I have ever met—but incapable. They kind of go insane because they have to keep pushing away the contradictions.

The only thing that ever happened in this town was that the whites stopped calling you niggers openly. And for years, the whole idea has been to avoid any confrontation that would cause you to be openly discriminated against or called a nigger.

In that community, Mrs. Younge—Sammy's mother—stood out as a person who might avoid clashing with white society whenever possible but who, if pushed, would stand up for her dignity.

MRS. YOUNGE: One of the first things I did in Tuskegee was to decide that I would never have a charge account at any small store because right off they would start calling you by your first name. When they did that—they couldn't pronounce it, in the first place—I would just ignore them. One time, a woman asked me, "What is your first name?" I felt like saying, "There wouldn't be any point in my writing it down because you wouldn't be able to read it." But I just said something about "There wouldn't be any point in my telling you because you wouldn't recognize it." She became very incensed, and I complained to the manager. After that, every time I came in the store the woman who owned it would wait on me.

Perhaps this was our only weapon, something to satisfy your pride or whatever. Just to set them in their place. It's something we latched on to, but it's just a thing. I know that my writing "Mrs." in front of my name is not going to make *them* call me "Mrs." if they care to call me by my first name.

Mrs. Younge's position in the community was complicated by her light color. The fact that she could "pass" affected her relations with black as well as white people. In a small town like Tuskegee, with its stifling, status-conscious atmosphere and its rampant gossip, she had to be particularly careful on this score. Yet here again she demonstrated a strong and forthright spirit.

MRS. YOUNGE: The fact is, I've had more trouble trying to be colored than white. I've been on trains and elevators and in many cases they wanted to usher me into the white coach or onto the white side. And when I refused, they got more angry with me than with colored people. Should I wear a sign?

I've always wanted to live where I could say hello to any friend; if I had to be in a situation where I would have to ignore a friend, I wouldn't feel comfortable. In Montgomery, not too long ago, I went down there to shop and I was with a friend of mine who is brown-skinned. I asked where the bathroom was. The woman said, "Right over there." So I asked, "Are those facilities open to both myself and my friend?" She said, "Oh, the bathroom for colored —that's right around the corner."

I have to be very careful of what I say to people who are brown or dark brown. They tell me, about using the word "nigger," "Look, you can't use that word." I don't like the word "nigger" but I'd call myself that. I've done that. It means so many things; it has so many connotations within our own race.

See, I understand myself. One day in the kitchen, my husband told me, "They're going to have a mass meeting." And I said, "Honey, I don't need anybody to get up and preach to me about what I'm gonna do." Now if you want the emotional part of it, the rallying and all of it—that may be necessary for some people. But it is not necessary for me to go and listen to a speech to know what's right. There are a few things I have seen that were wrong, and I haven't taken a step. So maybe movements are necessary, but I think the individual can pressure as well as a group. This has been my way. *All I'm trying to say is, Sammy came from people who always fought back with whatever means were available in their time and place.*

III "Lemon Younge"

Sammy Younge, Jr., was born in Tuskegee on November 17, 1944. His early life was in many ways like that of any bright, energetic kid who may misbehave but at the same time has a deep desire to make his family proud of him. Those closest to him in childhood were his mother and two friends his own age, Mrs. Washington's daughter, Laly, and Eldridge Burns. Another person who knew him as a boy was Doris Mitchell, a teacher.

LALY WASHINGTON: We were in nursery school together at the St. Joseph Catholic school. All I remember is what his mother and my mother told me. Like getting shots from a nurse, and Sammy and I would always complain about how she punched us in the arm. Then we would say bad things and have our mouths washed out with soap. Sammy was always getting into it with the Sisters.

ELDRIDGE BURNS: Sammy and I were in school together, starting with kindergarten at the Catholic school. We used to wear baseball suits to class, and every day after school we used to go up on campus to watch football practice. We'd hear people swearing, so we'd go back to school and say "damn" and "hell" all the time. I left the Catholic school and Sammy stayed, but we were still very close. Sammy wouldn't go to school some days. He'd say, "Aw, hell, they ain't teaching nothing—I know it all anyway."

MRS. YOUNGE: All the people in the community took an interest in him. We didn't have too many friends with children at that time so he would walk for blocks to play with other children. He was a child who never had to be provided for; he didn't need a Jack and Jill club. He liked to be out in the open and would ride a horse or something like that. Maybe because the other children weren't permitted to do those things, he was always kind of a loner when he was growing up. He loved anything with wheels on it. He'd have all kinds of cars, toys, some of which we bought and others that were handed down from other people in the family. He would ride them around the house and never bump into anything.

LALY WASHINGTON: Sammy loved to speed. When we were in elementary school, we'd go to the circus in Montgomery. My father was the man who took all the kids to the circus one year. He's a speed demon—he doesn't drive under ninety going anywhere. Sammy just loved this. He had all kinds of respect for "Uncle Bill." We stopped at the gas station, and my daddy told Sammy, who was sitting by the window, "You hold my coat while I go in here and get some cigarettes." Sammy was holding the coat out the window. Something happened, and he dropped it in the oil. Sammy jumped up and down in the seat and said, "Oh, Uncle Bill is going to kill me." He opened the door and picked up the coat and pulled it back in the car and tried to get the oil off. Of course it wouldn't come off. My daddy came back to the car and lectured Sammy all the way from the gas station to the circus. Sammy didn't say nothing. He just cried through the whole circus because he had messed up Big Bill's coat.

MRS. YOUNGE: He would come home with some of his problems. One time he had thrown a rock and broken a window of my neighbor's. He told me this—people didn't have to call in and tell me. I don't want to give the impression that we were always on Sammy's side. I don't mean he wasn't punished. Parents have certain ways and certain types of punishment. I never once tried to cover up for his weaknesses, and I don't think I ever let him down. And his father, too. That doesn't mean we've condoned all his actions.

DORIS MITCHELL: Sammy Younge was the only *free* middle-class child that I've ever seen grow up in Tuskegee. He was born into the largest of the middle-class families here, and he could have been a very snobbish and very uninteresting person, but his parents didn't squelch him into being something everyone else's children were. Sammy's mother never pressured him or his brother, Stevie. In the summer, Sammy was allowed to run around barefoot. Sometimes, when he was supposed to go to school, you'd see him playing and you would say, "Sammy, what are you doing outside?" He would answer, "I'm late for school, so I'm getting my recess."

Most middle-class Tuskegee people did not approve of going barefoot or any other conduct that might support the stereotypes about black people. But Mrs. Younge raised Sammy in her own proud, individualistic way.

MRS. YOUNGE: I didn't tell my children who to associate with. If I knew a child had a reputation for stealing, I'd never say, "Don't play with that person 'cause his momma is dirty" or something. I would say, "This is bad company to be in because if something happens, you are going to be labeled right along with the others." There are others who would turn up their noses at children from families where there's a lot of fighting and drinking and throwing things. But I'd just get them to play on the front porch of our house or out in the yard where I could be around.

Sammy might have made better grades in school if I had been pushing and demanding, if I had been like some parents that rewarded for higher grades and reprimanded for low grades. But all I ever said to him and his brother was, "I want you to do the best you can in any situation. I don't want you to fail, now that's for sure, because failure brings on unhappiness. But it's much more important that you learn something than that you get a grade. I don't want you to make an *A* in math and be unable to add six and eight and four. But I don't care if you make a *C* in math if you *can* add six and eight and four." Maybe this was my error . . . I don't know if young people always respond to this type of thing.

Sammy was unlike Stevie—Stevie would go to bed at three o'clock in the morning if it took that long for him to do his lessons. Sammy would do so much and say, "That woman gave me too much homework; I'm through with this." And he would go on to bed. But Stevie didn't have Sammy's exuberance, his urgency. Everything was so urgent to him. Things had to be moving, done now. Even as a little boy. When I had to take him someplace, I'd get him ready and before I could finish, he'd say, *"Come on, now, I got a long way to go and a little while to get there in."* He just always seemed to think that there was something he had to do, and he never knew how long he had to do it in.

MRS. WASHINGTON: He was much easier to manage if you put him in charge. Whenever we'd take a group of children together, we'd put Sammy in charge of the others. So I nicknamed him Big Shot. He loved this, being in charge. Our relationship was very warm. He was always anxious to do things that would make you happy. And always polite and agreeable. He was a restless child, but he would be very willing to listen if you didn't approve of something he'd done.

Sammy wasn't a talker; he might give you a one-sentence thing on something that disturbed him, but not a discussion. I don't recall any racial incidents. As a matter of fact, I don't really know what gave him the strong drive to become involved.

Sammy, like his mother, was very light-skinned. From childhood, this added complexity to his life just as his mother's color had made her situation in Tuskegee particularly sensitive.

MRS. YOUNGE: White children used to rush up to play with Sammy at the store. I never ran up and snatched him away. And everything would go all right until somebody came in the store. Then I would say, "Sammy, come here." I never made any issue of it, any deep explanation of it. I would just call him and interest him in something else.

One Saturday, I went to the store, and I happened to be the only one in there. The woman who normally ran the store must have been ill or something, and her husband was there. It was the first time I remembered seeing this man. We struck up a conversation. He told me what a handsome child I had; I said, "Thank you." And finally he got so talkative, he said, "Why you must bring your son down to play with my little daughter." So I said, "Thank you." Then a student of mine came in and I greeted her and started talking to her. That man turned red as a beet. I've seen him on the street since and he's looked the other way.

That day, Sammy probably felt something was wrong without knowing what or why. But the reality of racism was always there, waiting for him to discover it. Every black child has a first, conscious encounter with his own blackness and what it means in a racist, white-dominated society, although he may later forget the actual incident. We are not born knowing that we are black, and what that means. We must learn it. We must be taught that black is dirty and white means clean; about white angels, black devils; white dresses for virginity when one marries and enters a new life full of promise, but black when someone dies and enters the fearful unknown; a "black day" when things go wrong—and all the hundreds of other equations of black with evil, white with good, which our people today are uprooting and sometimes reversing: Black is Beautiful.

Sammy's first encounter came when he was about six or seven. Mrs. Younge recalled that she had taken Sammy to a children's party at the school in Tuskegee where she was then teaching. The children, between five and eight years of age, began to tease Sammy, calling him white. Not understanding why they did that, or exactly what it meant, he insisted that his mother explain after they left. Most black parents have to explain racism, but many of them try to shield their children from reality. Mrs. Younge talked to Sammy honestly about some of the complexities of race, assuring him that he was black and not white despite the color of his skin.

No one knows the full impact of that first discovery. But Sammy demonstrated his new consciousness in various ways after the incident.

LALY WASHINGTON: When I was about ten or eleven, our parents would go to Montgomery to shop together. Sammy and I would go roaming around the dime store. We used to play little games together. Sammy looked like he was white so he would go around one corner, and I would go around another corner, and we'd meet and embrace each other and say hello and all this kind of stuff. People would stop and stare and wonder what the devil was going on—you know, what is this white boy doing hugging this little colored girl? Of course, we never told our parents.

In the afternoon, we'd all meet back in a certain place at a certain time—say, in the Negroes' dining room in Walgreen's. Sammy and I would get loud and boisterous about colored water. We just hollered out, "What is colored water, Mama? What do they mean, colored water? I want some colored water." Our parents were poking us in the ribs and saying "Shh." Sammy and I would continue saying, "What in the devil is colored water? We want to know what colored water is?" So our parents would grab us and rush us into the elevator and then lecture us half-way from Montgomery to Tuskegee about making spectacles of ourselves.

Sammy thus chose to assert his blackness rather than to hide it, to confront white society rather than accommodate it. His little tricks were a way of attacking the racism which made it desirable for some blacks to pass. He was fighting for his identity, fighting to be black. That he chose to do so was largely the result of his mother's influence. Though she never told him about her aristocratic, Charleston heritage—"people who depend on family background for strength are very insecure," Mrs. Younge believed—she must have communicated a general sense of dignity to Sammy. She conveyed to him the idea that blackness was a cause not for shame or fear, but for pride.

LALY WASHINGTON: I remember once we were going somewhere on the train, maybe to Atlanta. We got on the train, and the conductor told Sammy's mother and Sammy to go to the left and told my mother and me to go to the right. Sammy's mother got very indignant. She said, "I know where I'm supposed to go and I'm going there." The conductor and she kind of argued. Sammy and I laughed about it, and we talked about it.

A turning-point in Sammy's life came when he was twelve and, for the first time, left the warmth of his home and community. At the beginning, he seemed happy—even exuberant.

MRS. YOUNGE: When Sammy finished the seventh grade, he went away to Cornwall Academy in Great Barrington, Massachusetts, for two years. It was no status thing with me. I had gone to private schools myself and I just felt that it would be the better type of education. I'm old-fashioned enough to believe that there's a quality of work that you don't get in public schools, and much more personal interest in the students.

ELDRIDGE BURNS: The teachers said that he had a good brain—send that boy off to a good school. Somebody had the same conception about me, so I went to another school about ninety miles from there. Sammy and I used to meet on weekends, but the big thing was train trips coming home. We were about fourteen then, and we always used to meet at Penn Station in New York City to take the train to Washington.

There was a conductor on the train who was Sammy's

Uncle Joe so we used to eat free coming home. Sammy would tell everybody on the train, "My name is Samuel Leamon Younge." "Leamon" was too hard to pronounce, and Uncle Joe used to say "Lemon." So we started calling him Lemon, Lemon Younge. And Sammy used to say, "I'm proud!" all the time. He'd just start yelling out, "I'm so proud," all over the train, and "Yeoee, yippie!" and all that kind of thing. Sammy was known all the way from New York to Alabama.

Sammy's race-consciousness grew stronger in the predominantly white world of the North, where the peculiar shelter of Tuskegee was lacking. Under this new pressure, he sometimes played his old tricks with whites and sometimes he also challenged their racism directly.

LALY WASHINGTON: I can remember a letter I got from him when he was at Cornwall Academy about how he didn't like it and that white people were getting on his nerves. He really had this strong thing. Also, he just wasn't very interested in school.

I went to the Howard School for Girls in West Bridgewater, Massachusetts, when he was at Cornwall. We'd meet in New York sometimes on the way home from school, and we'd play like we were madly in love. People really were wondering what was going on—this colored girl with this white boy—just like when we had gone shopping in the dime store as children. During my second year, Sammy and I were at the train station in Montgomery. I was on my way back to school. We went to this little white restaurant across the street from the station. We both put on Spanish accents, so the people thought I was Puerto

Rican or that we both were. Then we ordered a glass of milk and we talked with this little Spanish accent. The man looked at us kind of funny, but he brought the milk. We drank it, and then we said in plain old English, "Oh, thank you very much." In very clear, colored language, you know.

Other times, a couple of guys used to go someplace like Tick Tock's or Krystal's in Montgomery. Sammy would go in alone and with a very Southern accent he would order hamburgers for himself and his friends. The chick would bring the hamburgers and set them up on the counter and then all these Negroes would bop in.

MRS. YOUNGE: One time, he was coming down from school on the train and he went to the dining car. Somebody said, "Oh, we're getting near Tuskegee—this is the town where those niggers have taken over, boycotting." (This was at the time of the boycott.) When he got through eating, Sammy stood up and said, "I'm from Tuskegee, and I'm a Negro. My parents are boycotting." He said they just turned red, and then he walked out. He was fourteen years old then.

ELDRIDGE BURNS: When we would get on the train in Washington for Atlanta, Sammy used to say, "If the conductor tells you to go left, go right, because if you go left he's going to put all the niggers in that coach." The conductor told us to go left, so we went right. The conductor said, "Boy, I'll kick you off this train," and *Sammy pulled out his hairbrush and told him he was going to hit him.* That was the first time I realized how much he cared about the thing.

In his third year at Cornwall, Sammy's schoolwork began to suffer from the tensions he felt.

MRS. YOUNGE: His grades dropped from the 80's to the 60's. Sammy's teacher was from Miami; this might have been part of his problem. He might have looked for something because this person was a Southerner. Anyway, Sammy told me that the teacher was embarrassing this Jewish boy, and Sammy took it up. And the teacher looked at him and said, "Well, you know we don't have to tolerate you either." He said, "Yes, you do. As long as my parents continue to pay my bills, and I choose to stay here. But I don't know if I choose to stay here."

Then Sammy goes to Mr. Moran, the head of the school, and tells him that the teacher said Sammy was there just by their goodness in permitting a Negro to come. Just like they don't have to tolerate Jews, they don't have to tolerate Negroes. He was pushing Mr. Moran like mad to say who was right and who was wrong. He always did that. He was not a middle-ground person.

Sammy had a kind of inborn respect for human beings. He didn't always want you to agree with him, but he did want you to listen, to recognize him as a human being. If you didn't, he could be very rude without realizing it. It didn't have to be *his* cause; he just had a very, very keen feeling about treating people right. He couldn't stand innuendoes and sarcasm: he was not a child that you could bump around.

He had other trouble at Cornwall. He was suspended once for buying some beer. But those are things that boys will do. The real trouble, I believe, was what happened with the teacher. Sammy finally got to where I was worried that he might just walk off from school and I wouldn't know where he was. We sent for him; we sent his railroad fare. I think Mr. Moran was trying to hold him there, but Sammy just walked off one day. He was through with that situation, and he would have done it whether he had the fare to come home or not.

Sammy had learned two lessons at Cornwall: that being black is supposedly a bad thing in the U.S.A., and that wherever you go in this country, you are still black. Back home, Sammy entered Tuskegee Institute High School. But his problems were by no means over.

MRS. YOUNGE: Many people decided that he had been kicked out of Cornwall, that he was a juvenile delinquent. The teachers labeled him a hard child to handle. To me that was just ignorance.

When he came back, he really tried. In one of his courses, he was apparently not doing well, so I called the teacher and asked if there was anything his parents could do to help him. "That boy! Nobody can help him," the teacher said. I asked, "What do you mean?" And she said, "One of his friends told me that if I could corral him, I'd be the first one in the community who could ever do it. He's nothing but a juvenile delinquent." She had let one of his peers color her whole thinking. But you can't meddle with ignorant people in high places, not when they have your children under control.

Under the mounting pressures, Sammy found new ways to work off steam and new friends like Wendy Paris, another renegade from the Tuskegee middle class.

ELDRIDGE BURNS: Sammy's father had an old black Dodge, so we thought we knew how to drive. He used to park it out at the Veterans' Administration Hospital where he worked. We used to steal the car, take it out by the back gate, and go drive it out to Chehaw. One day we were seen by a patient who knew Sammy's father. So after we got to Chehaw, this cop stopped us. I think we were fourteen, and they took us to jail. We had to call our parents; they came and got us.

WENDY PARIS: I guess I first met Sammy during the summer of '59. I had a motorcycle, a small motorcycle, before that was "in." One day I was riding with a friend of mine; I had the muffler off. Sammy was walking up the street with a lot of kids, right there by Dr. Foster's house. Sammy cursed me out for coming through there too fast or something. I cursed him back and went on. Next day or two, I was up on the campus with the motorcycle. Sammy came over: "Say, man, let me ride with you." I guess we rode all afternoon.

The next day, someone had stolen his brother Stevie's bicycle. He came up to the house that morning and said, "Look, man, I want you to help me locate my little brother's bicycle." I said, "Okay." So we jumped on the motorcycle. Just rode all morning. I guess you could say that our friendship developed from that. We'd go on the campus half a day and play some basketball, go to a party late at night somewhere. He was just like a brother. We slept in the same bed and got the same plate. You name it, we've done it. We used to haul off chickens for six dollars a load, see old pictures, ride to Birmingham. Sammy always wanted action.

LALY WASHINGTON: My junior year in high school, Sammy and I got much closer. Both of us had transferred back to Tuskegee. He was a senior at Tuskegee Institute High

School when I was a junior. We had a group in school called the Unbelievables—seven of us that ran around together. Sammy was always kind of the crazy one in the crowd—not crazy, just more outgoing than anybody else.

WENDY PARIS: When he first got his license to drive a car, we used to slip his old man's car from him, tell Mr. Younge we were going to church, and then drive to Montgomery. Ride down there ninety miles an hour and ride back by the time church was out. We did it almost every Sunday. I think during the time we were running together, especially after he got his license, we ran through—oh, about ten cars.

ELDRIDGE BURNS: He had an old '49 Dodge—no, it was a '32 Dodge—well, a real old *T* model. It would go about twenty miles an hour. I think he got that when he was about sixteen, working at the filling station. This one night we were having a party, so we'd gone out in the woods and gotten some corn liquor. Sammy tried to drink the whole gallon. We went back to the car, and there was Sammy laid out. Everyone was wondering, was he dead, because he wouldn't wake up. Everybody started pushing on him. So we took him home, and that night he said, "Well, man, I'm not going to ever drink any more in my life."

Along with the teenage escapades, Sammy continued his old game of putting-on the white world.

WENDY PARIS: Right after those Freedom Rides and things in 1961, we'd go in a bus station just to go in there. Or in the stores. One time, in Lowe's Department Store in Montgomery, Sammy walked up to the white folks and said, "Pardon me, but do you have a lavatory that I may use?"

They said, "Yes, yes, yes." Showed him around to the white one. So he came back laughing. "You nigger boys sure can't do what I do."

Sammy always dressed stylish. Whatever was in, he'd have. Didn't make no difference that it might go out next year. He'd worry about that next year. He'd walk down the street, singing, with his hands behind him, humming a little tune. Sometimes we'd go in a store and I'd play his servant. And he'd have all the money. "You like that, boy?" "Yessir, I like that." "You want me to buy it for you?" "Yessir, buy it for me." So he'd buy it, and we'd laugh about it.

ELDRIDGE BURNS: Down in Montgomery one day, Sammy had to get a new heel put on his shoe. We went to H.L. Green's. You sit down, they fix your heel, and you get up and go. They had a place for Negroes, and they had a place for whites. So Sammy sat down in the white place and he took off his shoes, and he was waving his feet all around, with these bright yellow socks on. And they didn't know. They just didn't know.

But Sammy was on the edge of crisis, unable to find himself, falling into the trap that awaited many other young people in Tuskegee.

LALY WASHINGTON: One Sunday my father let me have this Cadillac. Sammy wasn't used to driving a Cadillac, and I wasn't either. This other girl had her Chevrolet station wagon and a whole bunch of kids were in her car. We went down Howard Road and Sammy started drag-racing. He put a big dent in my daddy's Cadillac. Of course, I had to say I did it. Sammy had been in trouble with the law about fast driving and reckless driving. Sammy was upset because I had to tell this lie, and he really didn't want me to do it. So I told him that it would be best that way because my father's insurance would cover me.

The next day, Sammy came over to my house, and I had just gotten home from school. Sammy said, "I want to talk to you." We had a soul session. He said, "Laly, I'm really worried." I asked him, "What's wrong?" He said, "What I really came by here for was to tell you how sorry I am that you had to lie to your mother. That was my responsibility and you shouldn't have done that." I told him it was okay. That he was like a member of the family and that it didn't make any difference. That the insurance would take care of it. I saw that he wanted to talk and that he was really upset about something.

He said, "Laly, I just don't know where I'm going. I don't know what I'm doing. I'm confused and things are not going right. I want to go to college, but I really think I can't make it. That's just not where it's at." We sat there for about three hours and he told me all about everything that had been going through his head. About how his mother was so sweet to him and would let him have anything he wanted and how he didn't feel he was living up to what they wanted him to be. About how he was influencing his little brother Stevie, and he didn't want Stevie to be anything like him. He went on to say that he realized he had made a lot of mistakes. That he didn't obey and all that kind of stuff. That he had caused his parents a lot of trouble, and he wanted to do something to make them proud of him.

Naturally he went on to talk about some girl. It seemed the only girls he got interested in were girls that someone else was interested in. Sammy had gone with Thelma once and with Mildred once. Now he was going with Veda. We talked about all this. He said he really didn't know what he was looking for in a woman. He didn't know if he would ever fall in love. It seemed as if every time he fell in love, something would happen. It didn't work out, and he didn't know. He wanted some children, but he didn't know.

Finally, he said, "I'm just going to play it by ear and see what happens."

IV　*Up-Tight*

　　As his graduation from high school drew near,
Sammy's dilemma became acute. Although he never formulated his problem as a search for some kind of commitment
to an ideal, his occasional demonstrations of interest in
religion seemed to suggest that. Sammy just didn't know
what to do with his life at this point, but he was fairly clear
about what he did not want to do.

LALY WASHINGTON:　We used to have a lot of discussions
about religion, a subject I don't think he discussed with too
many people. He had been confirmed a Catholic, but the
only time I saw him in the church was at his confirmation.
My mother would call Sammy at ten o'clock in the morning
and say, "Sammy, do you want to go to church with Laly
today?" Sammy would say, "Yeah, I'd be glad to go. I'm
going. I'm going." And I'd go by his house and he would
be asleep.

WENDY PARIS:　I almost likely got Sammy to join Reverend Holiday's church, a Baptist church. But then he went
over to Reverend Morris' church. They had a deacon
there, always in the Amen corner. Sammy used to like to
hear that man raise all that cane, "Amen, A-men," and
Sammy'd come back saying the same thing.
　　Reverend Morris was trying to get him to join that
church. Sammy was kind of skeptical. He'd say there was
no need, 'cause he'd seen these preachers drinking and cussing and everything. "That man no better than me. Ain't no
need in me joining this church." That's the one question we
never could answer.

LALY WASHINGTON: He said the church just wasn't for
him. He didn't want to go to college either. I said, "All
those private schools and all that good background, why
don't you want to use it?" Sammy said, "I just don't want
to go."

WENDY PARIS: They all wanted him to go to school. He
wanted to go in the Navy. We'd be riding around in his
car, and he'd say, "Man, I'm going in the Navy." If he said
something, that was it. So he went on in, in June of 1962.

   One of the ways for any frustrated young man to deal
with his problems has always been to "join the Navy and
see the world." That many black youths do this is not
surprising when one considers the patriotism instilled by
the educational system of the United States from the first
grade on: saluting the flag every day, joining the Cub
Scouts, the Boy Scouts, ROTC. Combine those influences
with the absence or distortion of our history as a black
people in the United States, the attempts to fragmentize
and downgrade our ties with the African continent, and
you have black children who grow up fiercely believing
that they are regular Americans who must fight to protect
this racist country.
   But Sammy's decision was unusual in one sense, for
the sons and daughters of the Tuskegee middle class usually
go straight on to college after finishing high school. They
do not interrupt their education. In order to survive in the
United States, the story goes, one must have a college education and advanced training in medicine or some other
profession. How else can one make money to live com-
fortably, own a home and two cars, and send one's children

in turn to college? By going into the Navy, Sammy Younge rejected that pattern of life.

Sammy signed up for three years, on active reserve status. After boot training, he was assigned for a while to the U.S.S. "Independence," an aircraft-carrier which then formed part of the American forces blockading Cuba. We do not know his opinion of the blockade itself, but it would have been normal—given the brain-washing of black school children mentioned above—for him to have accepted any American foreign policy as righteous. After that assignment, he came back to Portsmouth, Virginia.

During those first eight months in the Navy, Sammy maintained close ties with Tuskegee. He wrote letters and cards to different people, sometimes surprisingly casual acquaintances—like the owners of a gas station where he had worked before joining the Navy—with his remembrance. He would come back to Tuskegee on leave and also every weekend while stationed at Portsmouth, although it was a thirteen-to-fourteen-hour drive each way. He talked little about the Navy on these visits; mostly, he was just being Sammy and knocking around with old friends.

WENDY PARIS: When he'd come home, first thing he'd do is drive up and holler. We had that thing; we'd always holler "Whooooo." I guess we got that from calling cows on the farm and stuff. Very seldom I'd call him by his name. He might walk in the house and say "Hey, boy," or "What's happening, baby?" And that was it. We just had that inner feeling, that we knew there was a closeness. My house was just like his home away from home. He used to come over all times of the night or day and just eat or sit up and watch television.

Some people found him happy to be in the Navy and not particularly concerned about the issue of race. Certain words and actions, however, showed that his long-standing sensitivity was still there.

MRS. YOUNGE: When Sammy went into the Navy, I don't think there were a lot of racial issues. It was just a new-found freedom. He didn't speak to me about any mistreatment in the Navy. I don't think white people made too much difference to him then. Every time he came down here, he rode as far as Atlanta with a bunch of whites. He didn't have this thing that because you were white, you were nothing. He would accept you if he made up his mind that you were true-blue.

LALY WASHINGTON: In the first letters I got from him, he was just as happy as he could be. He was learning a lot about people. Of course, he was associating solely with the Negroes and criticizing the whites all the time.

WENDY PARIS: One time, when he came home on leave, we were out on the Montgomery Highway, riding and riding. We got to Chewacla State Park. He said, "Man, let's go up in here today." Okay. We'd been up in there plenty of times before, but Sammy was driving every time before. So we went on up in there, rode around looking. They got some beautiful scenery up there. We threw some rocks, went down by the creek bank, played down there a little while. We were driving all around, speaking to all the white people. We met this man in this truck and he was shaking this stick at us, cussing us and everything. Sammy said, "Let's go, man. Let's go." Then the Park Commissioner drove his truck up alongside of us and I had to pull over.

"What you niggers riding through here for?" the Park Commissioner asked us. Sammy didn't say nothing. I wouldn't say too much. Sammy never did much talking around white folks. I mean, 'til he knew, 'til we had a big group or something. He'd talk out then. That man had the upper hand, and he had a billy club. So we was kind of cooling it.

"Well, we just riding on through here."

"You know the laws of the State of Alabama," he said. "You can't ride through here."

"No, this is state property, man. We pay taxes and we ought to be able to ride through here."

The man wanted to argue that we were from Tuskegee, meaning uppity, and that we just wanted to start something. He charged us both with reckless driving. But when we arrived at the police station, Sammy asked, "How can I be charged with reckless driving when I wasn't driving?" So they locked me up. Sammy drove the truck in and called my mother. She came and got me, quick as she could. We rode back and laughed about it. Went on in there the next Sunday. The Park Commissioner didn't bother us that time.

While serving on the U.S.S. "Independence," Sammy had written his mother about the hard work he was doing, such as the constant swinging of very heavy mops to clean the decks. After his return ashore, he began complaining of a severe backache. He went often to the doctor at the Norfolk Base but no diagnosis was made. Finally, X-rays were ordered and still no diagnosis. Then, one night in September, 1963, he fell desperately ill and was rushed to the hospital in Portsmouth for emergency surgery. One of the openings in his left kidney had closed and poisons were backing up into his system. Both parents went to be with him. The doctor had informed them that the kidney had to be removed, and it would be a very dangerous operation. Mrs. Younge felt Sammy was going to die.

But the operation proved successful. According to the doctors, the malfunctioning of the kidney was congenital, but proper diagnosis and surgery at an earlier date could have prevented the kidney poisoning which had developed. Some medical error or inefficiency had apparently been committed.

This entire experience was frightening enough; then, four months later, Sammy had to have another operation. The malfunctioning of the bad kidney had impaired the other. Mrs. Younge again rushed to Portsmouth, where her son was still recuperating from the first operation. A second delicate operation was performed, and the other kidney was saved. The doctors warned, however, that Sammy would have to be very careful about his activities and avoid any injury to his right side. He even had to avoid catching a cold.

From the time of his first operation in September, 1963, until the middle of the following year, Sammy was forced to be virtually inactive. He was kept at Portsmouth, under constant observation, although he was able to come home occasionally on leave or passes. In July, 1964, the Navy gave him a medical discharge.

Later in the summer of 1964, Sammy went to work as a nursing assistant at the Veterans' Hospital in Tuskegee. Then, and into the fall, he continued to struggle with the same problems he had had before going into the Navy, but now there was a new problem—the constant threat of death. The operations themselves also haunted him. Friends told of how he would scream in his sleep, "Don't cut me any more! Don't cut me!"

In January, 1965, Sammy enrolled at Tuskegee Institute. But he didn't "settle down," as some had hoped. He was worried about his health, yet he was also foolhardy. He was troubled about the reputation he had acquired as a "bad boy," yet he was also defiant. More than anything else, Sammy seemed to be waiting for a solution that was out there, somewhere.

ELDRIDGE BURNS: Sammy was very smart, but he didn't care about things as important-but-unimportant as school. He cared, but he never could sit still. He had to get in a car and just drive up and down the road. Then he'd come back and stay for five minutes and then drive up and down the road again.

We were very tight, very close friends, but he always used to get mad at me when I would start talking to him about what he should be doing. You know, Sammy had only one kidney and that one was bad, so he couldn't drink hard liquor or beer. But he still liked to drink wine. He was the only man I knew who could leave the house at 6:28 and make it to the liquor store before it closed at 6:30. We'd go get wine, and we'd start drinking. I knew he had pains, and I'd say, "Sammy, you'd better cut it out." He would get mad and say, "Well, I'll see you," and go on home or some place else. Then later on that night he'd come back. He'd sit out in the car and start talking about how he knew it was wrong, but he just wanted people to leave him alone 'cause he was going to do right. He was going to be okay.

V   The Toilet Revolution: First Day

A long line of students from Tuskegee Institute marched for two blocks and then filed into the wide street in downtown Montgomery. They were walking quietly toward the gleaming white Capitol of Alabama, where white people carried on the business of Alabama for black and white people—and where the business of the white Governor, George Wallace, was keeping blacks in their place. It was Wednesday, March 10, 1965.

The students brought with them a petition protesting two things: the denial of voting rights to black people, and the brutal beating of civil-rights demonstrators at the Pettus Bridge in Selma on the previous Sunday, when they attempted to march from Selma to Montgomery. There were more than seven hundred students together with their teachers and some staff members of the Student Nonviolent Coordinating Committee. For most of the Tuskegee people, this was their first organized demonstration against white supremacy.

They stopped at the yellow barricades erected by the police. Behind the barricades stood long lines of Alabama state troopers with their huge redneck frames, looking mean. The Montgomery County posse sat on horseback swinging their long nightsticks; the horses were eager, taut, waiting to be spurred to tromp on the black students, as they had in 1960 when students from Alabama State College had protested in front of the Capitol. Not until this day, some five years later, had whites again witnessed black people standing before the Capitol with a petition in their hands.

With them stood Sammy Younge. That day would change his life and the lives of some of his fellow students. Until then, Sammy had been a very young man—barely out of his teens—with problems typical of his age and typical of black middle-class youth. After that day, the whole context of his life altered; his problems were not fully solved but they took on a new focus.

March 10, 1965, was also the first time I met Sammy Younge. As an officer of SNCC, I found myself very involved in the Montgomery demonstration—far more than anticipated. Therefore, in explaining what happened at the Capitol and afterward, I will comment frankly on my own participation and also on certain developments within the Movement in Alabama. The surface events of that day must be seen in relation to the deeper political currents swirling around Sammy and the other Tuskegee students.

The story actually begins two years before. In early 1963, SNCC had started a voter-registration project centered around Selma, the seat of Dallas County. On October 7 of that year, the first "Freedom Day" in SNCC's history took place in Selma; large numbers of Negroes gathered at the courthouse to register while others picketed in support. That effort led to the first major confrontation with Dallas County's notorious Sheriff Jim Clark. It would take two years to break his terroristic stranglehold through several federal suits and the organization of black people which grew out of our intensive work in the area.

For the summer of 1964, it was anticipated that we would work on an Alabama project with the Southern Christian Leadership Conference, headed by Dr. Martin Luther King, Jr. But SCLC went to St. Augustine, Florida, instead, despite the urging of some of its staff to carry out the Alabama plan. At the end of 1964, however, SCLC's interest in winning the vote in Alabama revived, partly be-

cause of encouragement from the national Democratic
Party, which had been disturbed by Johnson's failure to
carry several Southern states in the November election and
which wished to develop new Democratic voter strength.
SCLC thus decided to devote almost all of its organizational
energy to a massive right-to-vote campaign, with headquar-
ters in Selma. SNCC, already based in Selma, agreed to cooperate in this new venture, and the campaign officially
began on January 18, 1965. But disagreement on such key
issues as concepts of leadership, working methods, and organizing voters for independent political action versus
Democratic Party politics, bred conflict between SNCC
and SCLC staffs in Alabama.

As the vote campaign intensified, accompanied by in-
numerable arrests and beatings, the proposal emerged for a
march on the Alabama Capitol to demand the vote, as well
as new state elections. Basically SNCC was opposed to a
Selma-Montgomery march because of the likelihood of police brutality, the drain on resources, and the frustrations
experienced in working with SCLC. At a lengthy meeting
of its executive committee on March 5 and 6, SNCC voted
not to participate organizationally in the march scheduled
for Sunday, March 7. However, it encouraged SNCC staffers to do so on a non-organizational basis if they so desired.
SNCC was also to make available radios, telephone lines,
and certain other facilities already committed by our Alabama staff.

Then we heard that Dr. King would not appear at the
march he himself had called. Without his newsworthy presence, it seemed likely that the lives of many black people
would be even more endangered. We therefore mobilized
three carloads of staff workers from Mississippi, two-way
radios, and other protective equipment. At our national office in Atlanta, a group of SNCC people—including Ala-

bama project director Silas Norman and Stokely Carmichael, whose subsequent election as SNCC chairman
was largely the result of his work in Alabama—chartered
a plane rather than make the five-hour drive to Selma.
Since we had heard of King's absence only after the marchers had begun to assemble, none of SNCC's people was
able to arrive for the march itself. But it seemed important
to have maximum support in the event that violence developed that evening. While our various forces headed for
Selma, we tried repeatedly, but unsuccessfully, to contact
Dr. King, to find out his reasons for not appearing and to
discuss the situation.

Our fears proved all too well-founded: hundreds, including SNCC chairman John Lewis, were beaten,
whipped, and tear-gassed by Jim Clark's deputies and Alabama state troopers at the bridge that Sunday.

A new attempt to march was scheduled for the following Tuesday; SCLC also filed a suit seeking to enjoin the
Alabama Highway Patrol and Sheriff Jim Clark from inter-
fering with the march. I arrived in Montgomery early Monday evening and found James Farmer, then director of
CORE, also at the airport. A. D. King, Martin's brother,
told us that we were wanted at a meeting. Gathered there
were Martin Luther King, Ralph Abernathy, Andrew
Young, Hosea Williams, and Bernard Lee of SCLC, together with Fred Gray and Solomon Seay, Jr., Montgomery attorneys.

Farmer and I were informed that Judge Frank Johnson of the Federal Court of the Middle District had promised the SCLC lawyers that if Tuesday's march from Selma
to Montgomery was canceled, he would hold a hearing
Thursday on the injunction suit which SCLC had filed.
Judge Johnson's other conditions were that there be no
demonstrations in Montgomery and that the march not pro-

ceed in any way before or during the hearing. He expected
an answer by 9:00 P.M., said Fred Gray.

The group assembled wanted to know what James
Farmer and I had to say. It was clear that the consensus was
to accept Judge Johnson's offer; Hosea Williams was the
only SCLC leader pushing for the march. Farmer stated
that, while he had come down to march and emotionally
understood the position of Hosea, rationally he had to agree
with waiting until Thursday. I stated that, first, I had not
come to march and, second, I had not yet talked with our
Alabama staff, so none of my remarks could be binding.
With these reservations, I offered my analysis of the situation: that the Judge's offer was legal blackmail. There was
no guarantee of getting the injunction and no deadline for
the completion of hearings on it. "So many times in the
past," I added, "we have seen movements killed by placing
the question in the courts, waiting for weeks or months to
get an injunction—or just a hearing on one."

Martin Luther King decided to accept the Judge's
condition. The march would be postponed.

The entire group left immediately for Brown's Chapel
in Selma. There, to my amazement, King pledged before a
mass meeting that the march would begin the next morning
at eight o'clock!

Not having had a chance to talk with the SNCC staff,
I decided not to raise any questions about King's announcement publicly. When asked to speak, I talked about the
need for organizing politically when the vote was won. Immediately afterward, I met with the SNCC staff who were
disturbed to hear of the way people had been misled.

Later, SCLC held a meeting to reconsider the decision
against marching; the SNCC staff attended. After three
hours, Dr. King was convinced that he should reverse his
position. He telephoned Attorney General Nicholas Katz-

enbach at 4:30 A.M. to tell him that the march would proceed. According to King, they talked over forty-five minutes and Katzenbach was angry. "I really had to preach to him," said King. I then decided to participate in the march, as King urged, hoping that events might continue to move him away from the U.S. government. Developments in the years which followed, and in particular Dr. King's stand on the Vietnam war, indicate that this did take place to a considerable degree.

As we had anticipated, Judge Johnson issued a court order a few hours later against the march or any type of demonstration. Katzenbach had not sat idly by. But we knew it was impossible to enjoin a whole town and we also felt that, at this point, people had to move. We therefore urged that anyone who had not actually been served papers under the court order should participate. (As we later learned, only three persons were named in the order.)

Hundreds stood ready to march, including many Northern supporters. But once again we were fooled. After crossing the bridge, going a few yards beyond the spot where people had been beaten on the previous Sunday, and then kneeling in prayer, Dr. King turned the march around and led it back to Selma. This was done, according to my own information and the press coverage of the time, in compliance with a "compromise" agreement made between the Administration and Dr. King through the intermediacy of LeRoy Collins, director of the Federal Community Relations Service. King did not inform the marchers of that agreement. Needless to say, people were dismayed, baffled, and angry.

Back in Selma, Dr. King stated that all marches in Selma or Montgomery would be postponed pending the outcome of the injunction suit. This was on Tuesday, March 9. Relations between SNCC and SCLC were at a very low point. We began holding meetings of the SNCC staff, as well as meetings between SNCC and SCLC, to resolve our difficulties. That night in Selma, local racists attacked three white ministers, one of whom—Reverend James Reeb—later died from the beating he received.

The ban on all marches upset plans already made for a demonstration the next day at the Capitol in Montgomery—the demonstration in which Tuskegee students, including Sammy Younge, were then planning to participate. Their march was not just another protest but the outcome of several months' work at Tuskegee. In the fall of 1964, SNCC had sent several "campus travelers," headed by Bill Hall, to help organize the students there. There had been little activity at the Institute up to that time. Encouraged by SNCC staffers, members of a campus organization called Tuskegee Institute Advancement League (TIAL) made trips to Selma to help in the voter-registration campaign. But student involvement remained limited and mostly on an individual basis. George Ware, one of the most active students, told me how the campus finally became mobilized and how that new awareness led to plans for action at the Capitol.

GEORGE WARE: Everybody had seen what happened on television, and there was a lot of talk about the beatings on that bridge. Tuskegee students felt that they should react somehow. King had called for people from all over the state to go to Montgomery and have a massive demonstration. So TIAL tried to mobilize students. We assigned two TIAL people to each dorm and went around to all the dormitories that Sunday night, talking about the need to get involved. We had a whole series of meetings. Just about all the people in the dorms turned out.

On Monday, we held a mass meeting to talk about this some more. People were agreeing to go, and getting very

enthusiastic. And the community in Tuskegee was not opposed to this, since it meant no action *in* Tuskegee. People
began contributing money, and Sammy Younge was placed
in charge of fund-raising for the whole campaign. The students took buckets and went all up and down in the campus
and the community talking about Selma, talking about Alabama justice and the need for some sort of reaction. People
contributed almost twelve hundred dollars over a two-day
period, enough for us to consider renting buses to take
students down there.

TIAL planned to go on Wednesday because it was for
that day King had put out the call for the Montgomery
demonstration. We had a big meeting the night before to
work out some of the logistics: to get the names of all those
who planned to go, and to try to get in touch with lawyers,
with people who could bail folks out if they went to jail.
That afternoon, Martin called a press conference in which
he called off that whole demonstration. He said, "No, we
will not have a caravan into the capital; we will wait."
Well, the TIAL people felt that they had put a lot of
energy into that march. And they also felt there was a
need for somebody to move, that what had happened in
Selma shouldn't be allowed to die.

So we had a caucus meeting, and we decided we were
going to go anyway. But we felt we had to be honest, so
we had a big meeting—I guess there were over a thousand
students there. I got up and said, "Dr. King has called the
whole thing off, but we are still going. Anyone who feels
that they don't want to go because of Dr. King's position
should leave now so that we can proceed to work out the
logistics. Because this is not a mass meeting to bring people
in, this is a meeting to handle the problems of all those who
are going." Only about ten people left.

There had been a lot of resistance to the students coming down there. We had called the head of the Montgomery Improvement Association, Reverend Douglas, to let him know we were coming. He got very angry and disturbed, and said that Dr. King had called it off. He said we shouldn't come down. There was also a telephone call that night to SCLC. They kept saying, "We've got this whole thing figured out. We know what we're doing. You all don't, so don't go down there." We said, "Okay, thank you very much," and continued to move. The next morning we had about four or five buses and an unbelievable number of cars. People were loaning us their cars to go down there.

Tuskegee student leaders and SNCC staff members told the story of what happened after that.

GEORGE WARE: We got seven hundred people to Montgomery. Now, we knew where everybody was supposed to meet according to King's original call. We decided to go to that church because from that point on, we would be feeling our way on a lot of things. So we began to arrive at the First Baptist Church early in the morning, about nine o'clock. The church was open; everybody went in.

Then Reverend Douglas came up and said, "Well, since you're all here and you all are gonna march, I'll be with you. But we don't have a parade permit."

"What can we do about that?" I said.

A detective came over. "You can't march without a permit."

"It takes two days to get a permit," he said.

We decided that if it was going to take two days, we would just have to march without one. Then he and the minister went downtown and got a permit in twenty minutes. Strangely enough, it said what time the parade was supposed to start, but nothing about when it was supposed to end. That turned out to be very important.

There was a lot of confusion, for the simple reason that we really didn't know what the hell we were doing, like, how do you keep that many people from getting disturbed about a lot of little things? There was a rumor that horses were being unloaded down at the stadium to mobilize against us. A lot of uneasiness and fear started building up inside that church. Finally, somebody got up and started talking about Selma and how we ought to respond in spite of the horses.

We had drawn up a petition and, in typical TIAL-SNCC fashion, we had run off and left it in Tuskegee. So there was the whole problem of drafting another petition in the church. I sat down for about fifteen minutes and got befuddled by the whole thing because there was so much else going on. We got some professors, told them what we wanted, and they drew it up in nice language.

Meanwhile, we had been joined by about three hundred people from the Montgomery area which included some students from Alabama State College and some general community people. So we had about a thousand people when we were ready to go out in the street. That was just before one o'clock. A funny thing happened then. All these ministers had sort of been against us from the beginning. They really didn't want the march because we were going against the wishes of Martin Luther King. But the minute we got outside, there were about twelve ministers standing at the front of the line. They had just appointed themselves the leaders of the march. But we wanted it to look like a student protest.

Earlier, we had called SNCC to make sure that they would be there, because we knew there might be a lot of problems that we couldn't handle. So now Bill Hall and some other SNCC people helped us get rid of the ministers. We told them just to mix freely with the students rather than to form a group of black ministers. They were very pissed off about that and said, "We're the local leaders and if you got something going on around here, we ought to be a part of it to give you some kind of protection. . . ." They had a lot of bullshit rationalizations for trying to lead that march.

After we got the ministers mixed up with the students, we started out. Some more SNCC people arrived midway through the march; Jim Forman was one of the persons who came in at about that time. As we started marching toward the Capitol, the police were out handling traffic and making sure it was an uncomplicated situation. The Montgomery police department had decided to let us have our march, get it off our chest, and get out of their city. It was obvious they wanted to play that role.

When we got to the Capitol, it was kind of a formidable scene. There must have been more than a hundred cops from the Montgomery police force lined up facing us and around us in a sort of U. Along the sidewalk in front of the Capitol, they had put up a barricade which divided city property from state property. The city cops were in front of the barricade. On the other side of it was Al Lingo, I think, and his state troopers, obviously very irritated about the whole thing.

LAURA PAYTON: When we got to the Capitol building, I remember feeling something like fear for just a few minutes. It came and left so suddenly that I never really thought about it. We went down and there were police on each side of us. That's when most of the people told me they really got nervous. We sat down and started singing some freedom songs again, which I liked. I had heard them for the first time in the church.

GEORGE WARE: George Davis and I were at the head of the march, and we had the petition. When we got up to the Capitol, we noticed that the press was all the way back on the lawn, way over to the right where they couldn't photograph or hear anything that was going on. The Assistant Chief of Police was standing there. "That's as far as you can go," he said. "I have no jurisdiction beyond this point."

"Anybody who crosses that line is not going to walk back on the other side again," said Mr. Lingo.

"I would like to read this petition," I said. "But I would like to read it so that the press can hear it. Why is the press all the way over there?"

"The state designated that place for them, and that's where they're going to have to stay," said Lingo.

So I read the petition to the group. And then we demanded that the Governor either come down or send a representative to accept the petition. The Chief of Police informed us that that wasn't about to happen, and we could forget about the whole thing. As far as he was concerned, he would hope that the Governor would do it, but it wasn't going to happen.

George Davis and I decided we'd go over and read the petition to the press. We started walking to where they were, and on the way a state detective came over and said, "Get on over there with your group. You don't have any business here."

"I'm on city property, and the Chief of Police said that I could go over there," I said.

"I don't give a damn what he said. Get back over there."

So I turned around, went back, and told the Chief of Police, "Look, man, are they on state property? Do you have jurisdiction there or not?"

"We don't want to get in a hassle with the state police," he said. "There's a press box halfway down the street. I'll send some pressmen down there, and you can talk." He was still our buddy then. So George Davis, Bill Hall, and I went to the press box.

That same detective was down there and he said, "I told you once, goddamit, to get the hell outa here, and if you don't leave I'm gonna put you in jail." The reporters split.

I looked over at George, and he looked at me, and I said, "Do you want to leave, man?" And he said, "Well, I don't know. . . ." And then I said, "Well, I guess we won't leave." So the cat arrested us and put us in the car. The minute he arrested us, the group which had been standing out there sat down. They said, "Well, if this is the way things are gonna be, we just gonna stay here."

The Chief of Police saw that it was a crisis. He called over the detective who had arrested us, started talking with him, and somehow negotiated our release. Then he said, "Now that we've got you out of trouble—'cause they were gonna take you downtown and beat your ass—why don't you sing a few songs and go on back to the church?" I told him, "Well, I don't have no argument with you about your role, but we came here to present a petition to the Governor. It seems to me that we ought to stay here and try to do that."

Now he called the ministers over and started to talk to them in a little caucus on the side. Some SNCC people were moving around near their group and saw that a deal was being made between the ministers and the city police. A minister came over to me. "Well, we talked with the

Chief of Police, and it's obvious that you aren't going to be able to present your petition. So why don't we, after a short while, just leave?"

"I don't think we ought to leave," I told him. There had been a lot of feeling and a lot of talk about staying there until the Governor saw fit to come down and take our petition.

"But you've got to, because I promised the Chief of Police that we all would be leaving here within an hour."

"Why do you say we have to leave 'cause you promised?" I asked him. "I didn't think that this was a ministers' thing in the first place. It was my idea that this was a student protest and it would be up to the group out there to decide whether they were going to leave."

We started talking with different people standing in different areas. George Davis, myself, Forman, Hardy Frye, and some other people started informal workshops around what to do. There was a lot of feeling for staying. People felt, "Okay. We'll stay, and we'll sit down here." Meanwhile, the police began to surround us.

WILLIE RICKS: The Man began to increase the pressure. And as the pressure increased, the ministers decided to say three prayers, sing one song, and then go home. So they prayed, and they sang, and they split.

GEORGE WARE: Then the whole question came up about the restroom. People had to go to the restroom. The Dexter Avenue Baptist Church was right down the street, so a group of people went down there. They found out that the church had been locked and would not be opened because the minister had said that we wouldn't listen to them. Now, when that group tried to come back, the police would not let them in. I went over and talked with the Chief of Police.

"What are you doing? Why are you restricting people?" He said, "I'm not restricting people. People can come and go as they want." For a while, people kept going out but not coming back in. And we finally discovered that he was allowing people to leave and saying that they could come back in, but he wasn't really letting anybody back through that line.

There began to be a lot of unrest on the part of the students and on the part of Dean Phillips [Bert Phillips, Dean of Students at Tuskegee Institute]. George Davis was talking to one group of people at one end, and I was talking to another segment. People began to say, "We can't stay here too long. We have to use the restroom. We are going to go back at five o'clock; that's the time the buses are supposed to pick everybody up. If we don't go then, we're stuck here." And then I really got hung up in a lot of questions of logistics. My position was that I wanted to stay, but if people wanted to leave, then okay, the hell with it.

After a lot of arguing among ourselves, we took a vote of the student body. The majority wanted to stay. Then Dean Phillips began talking about his responsibilities as Dean of Students, and he got into a thing with Forman. That started a whole other discussion. Finally Jim just said, "Fuck it. I'm going to stay," and went and sat down. About five hundred people left, about three hundred stayed [some had left earlier in the day]. I was thinking about my responsibility too, since I had something to do with the students coming down there. Sammy Younge was one of them encouraging others to stay.

Then the police really began to use a lot of weird tactics. It was beginning to get dark—it was after five—and the police said, "Well, you gonna have to leave because if you don't, we gonna have to rout you." People were singing freedom songs because they were getting pretty scared. At one point, when everybody was standing up, the police pulled back and formed a V-formation and they ran forward like an attack. The only thing that kept a lot of panic from breaking out was the fact that Jim Forman said, "Everybody sit down." People kind of responded to that 'cause there was no other suggestion of what to do. The cops ran right up to the group and stopped and it became obvious to us that they had never intended to run into that group. We laughed about that, and it reinforced a lot of our feelings about staying.

Then the Chief of Police came up and also a couple of pressmen. The Chief called me over and said, "Well, I've been very nice and I've tried to allow you to have your protest demonstration, but you're paralyzing over eighty per cent of my police force." He started that whole logical thing.

"The people decided to stay, man," I told him. "I don't have too much to say."

The reporter said, "You're being unfair to the police officer. Your fight is with the Governor."

"Well, it just happens that Montgomery is the capital," I answered, "and that's where we are."

Then the police tried another thing. "We gonna leave you here. There are Klansmen over there and if we leave you here some of you might get hurt, so you better go, 'cause we gonna leave you." We didn't bother to respond to that one way or the other. The police pulled off and went about half a block. When they saw that we weren't going to go, they came back and formed a group around us. They started a whole harassing thing. Every time people would stand up, the cops would move up as close as they could get, which made it very difficult for anybody to sit down. Then the cops said that people were bumping up against them and there were arguments. They were trying to use any excuse to start beating on people.

They brought a diesel engine which they were going to set up so that the fumes would come down over the group. But they couldn't get the diesel engine started so they went and got a jeep. They bent the exhaust thing in our direction and just sat there and roared the engine while the fumes wafted over the demonstrators.

Meantime, people had solved that problem about the restroom. They would take the picket signs and surround the person, and he would urinate and settle that whole question. That's how it got tagged a piss-in by white people. Because after about five hours of this, there was a constant stream of urine running down the hill. That made the cops kind of open up, because it was getting on their nerves.

People go through a lot of funny changes when they have to do something as personal as urinate. There were a lot of chicks who at the beginning couldn't conceive of doing anything like that; it really went against everything they'd ever been taught. There was one radical priest, a cat from the south part of Chicago, who held back all evening. He had his habit on and everything. He was saying, "Well, I really wish I could urinate." And I said, "Why don't you go on over there, man?" He said, "No, I can't do that." About 10:00 P.M. he came on over and said, "I'm sorry, man. I'm gonna have to do something." So he went on over and pulled up his habit and urinated. After that, he became a much nicer cat.

SNCC had brought up portable toilets and an ambulance from Selma had come up for people who had got sick from the fumes. But the police wouldn't let the toilets or the ambulance through. Fred Meely of SNCC had gone outside the lines to see about bringing medical supplies, but they wouldn't let him back in. He and three or four other people got arrested trying to get back. People were very depressed. Then Mrs. Lois Reeves started singing some crazy little song, and it kind of rejuvenated everybody's spirit. We were reconciled to the fact that we were going to stay all night.

VI The Toilet Revolution: Escalation

SNCC staffers had originally joined the students at Montgomery that day because we felt that we must radicalize the march, radicalize the students from middle-class Tuskegee. But if SNCC was to have any meaning to students, if it was to involve them in the Movement, it had to be with them at a particular moment. I saw the demonstration as a vital learning-experience and a basis for commitment. The only way to get the students involved, it seemed to me, was to get them in motion, try to make them militant, explain—for example—what those ministers were doing. In short, give them a cram course in civil-rights activity.

During the day, we had been able to remain by playing upon the contradictions and conflicts between the Montgomery police and the Alabama state troopers. We were in the jurisdiction of the city; if we had been in the jurisdiction of the state, we most certainly would have been long gone. The city police had offered protection because of Montgomery's image and, to some extent, because of the open-ended permit. Then their attitude changed. At the same time, it grew dark and very cold.

That night it was agreed that I should handle the situation. I had been reluctant to assume any kind of leadership, but now there was the question of how to control so many people—most of them exhausted and without coats. Then, about 1:00 A.M. it began to rain. We also realized that there's a limit: you could urinate in the street, but what would happen when people started defecating? We decided that the best thing was to use the rain as a situation for leaving. It was then about 2:00 A.M.

Reverend Johnson had told us that his church, First Baptist, would be closed to us. Dexter Avenue Baptist Church was just half a block down the street but it too was closed. We thought we might go to the Trailways Bus Station, but a detective said that there were a lot of hoodlums hanging around there, and that seemed likely because people had been beaten there in 1961. Finally we decided that we would go to the First Baptist Church anyway because it was only four or five blocks away and the bus station would have been a longer walk. When we got there, the doors somehow just opened and we walked in.

We spent that night sitting in the basement on the concrete floor, talking. Sammy was with us. Reverend Johnson came in about 3:00 A.M.; he wasn't pleased about our taking over his church. He wanted to have the women sleep upstairs and the men downstairs. But no one felt like hearing any nonsense about splitting up after what they had gone through with the police and all the discomfort. Finally he threw up his hands and said, "All right. You got my church." We told him we'd try to take care of it.

In the morning—it was now Thursday, March 11—he came back and said that we had to be out by 10:30. Meanwhile, the executive committee of TIAL had decided that all Tuskegee students should go back to the campus. Buses were already lining up; the Tuskegee administration had probably ordered them during the night. We in SNCC knew that we were going to lose a lot of people anyway, but that a hard core of activists would emerge from the situation. We therefore began by not challenging the TIAL decision: instead, we moved the discussion onto the more basic level of what was at stake, what long-range values were involved. People were torn asunder by the debate.

Sammy said at first that he wanted to stay. But then some people talked about the need for the Tuskegee student body to move as a unit, and he seemed to waver. Some said it was necessary to go back to Tuskegee and get more students. Bill Hall spoke about the need to develop strong people, not leaders, because a strong people needed no leaders—or at least did not need strong leaders. People began to leave. Sammy got on the bus and said to me, "Look, man, I'm going to go back and get some more people. I'll be back here Saturday."

Around noon, we moved from that church to the Dexter Avenue Baptist Church. Then Reverend James Bevel of SCLC arrived with a trustee of the church. Meanwhile, new groups of students arrived from Tuskegee and Alabama State. Also, a group came from the Montgomery Improvement Association, which is an SCLC affiliate. They were ready to go back to the Capitol that day. But Bevel, speaking first, talked about how disgraceful the urinating had been; how we were spoiling the nonviolent image; that what we were doing in Montgomery wasn't part of the plan for Alabama, which was focused on Selma. As I began to answer, Bevel sat down in the front row and started heckling—an old trick sometimes used by Baptist preachers at business meetings when they disagree with the speakers and want to disrupt the discussion. It worked.

The people in the room, like most students, were not concerned with internal squabbles but with the motion, the action, the plan. To have dealt with Bevel then, I would have had to review the whole history of King's actions in Selma. I decided to stop trying to talk and just continue with our plan. I was especially concerned about the students from Tuskegee who had remained; there was a very close bond developing between us.

Four SNCC people—Bill Hall, Stu House, George

Bess, and I—left the basement of the church, saying that we were going to the Capitol because that was what people had come to Montgomery to do. There were police blocking the church door, preventing the students from leaving. We managed to sneak through the line. As we reached the Capitol, we were turned back by a colonel and a captain of the highway patrol in their blue uniforms and Confederate gray overcoats. We tried to argue jurisdiction—that we were on city, not state, property—but they forced us back. When we tried to cross the street, we were stopped by the city police: "Arrest them! Arrest them!" All of us were dragged to the paddy wagon. At jail, I was put in solitary confinement.

Meanwhile, at the church, Bill Hall and James Granville were hit by the police as they tried to get past the barricade. A group of Tuskegee students decided to stay inside indefinitely. Earlier, the trustees of the church had said that they were going to close it and that everyone must leave; we had argued that the people had a right to stay there, that God meant for everybody to have a church, that the church belonged not to the trustees but to the people. The student group was now backing up those words with action.

In jail, we learned that people were staying in the church and decided that we should get bailed out in order to reinforce them. We felt that the church had become a key issue. In the South, many a preacher has blocked organizing efforts by refusing to make available his church, one of the few meeting places possible. In Mississippi, for example, it had been impossible to get a church for two-and-a-half years. Now, in Montgomery, the ministers were controlling the Movement by locking us out. The Dexter Avenue Baptist Church had particular importance; it was strategically located, facing the state Capitol. We could have a demonstration right on the church steps.

We succeeded in winning access to the Dexter Avenue Church just for that Thursday night. By then, I was so exhausted and feverish that a doctor came to the church, treated me, and advised me to sleep in the Ben Moore Hotel for an evening. The next morning, I returned to find the church barricaded by the police. No one could enter except Bevel, who was going in and out. On one occasion, we brought food for the people inside and asked him to take it in to them. He could at least do that. He refused, and left the food—about fifty dollars' worth—on the bottom step. The cops came after a while and threw it into the garbage can.

We were perhaps more furious with Bevel than with the police, and we went to see King in the Ben Moore Hotel to tell him what was going on. He had to take responsibility for his staff, we said. If we found Bevel in his hotel room, we told Martin, we were going to block the door and not let him out. We also urged King, as former pastor of the Dexter Avenue Baptist Church, to use his influence with the trustees. All we wanted them to do was to turn the water back on, so that people could use the toilet, and to assure us that we could use the church when we had demonstrations.

King said that he would try, but that we had to realize the ministers in Montgomery were not cooperating with the Movement generally. Those at the First Baptist Church, where Ralph Abernathy of SCLC had once pastored, had refused to let even SCLC use the church. The situation had become so bad, King pointed out, that SCLC itself was planning to sit-in at one of the churches. He therefore sympathized with us. He then added that some of the trustees had expressed concern about the maintenance of the church. We told him that we were unable to enter the church and therefore could not judge its condition, but we believed the people would make an effort to keep it clean. In any case, this argument struck us as a smoke screen for the trustees' unwillingness to cooperate.

That Friday evening, the entire board of deacons and a black federal marshal came to the church. They told the students that the police were going to leave at night and they would be at the mercy of Montgomery's white hoodlums. Soon afterward, but not because of that visit, those in the church decided to leave. I was not present, and the various reports I heard afterward never enabled me to understand the exact reasons for this decision.

The first semester of the Tuskegee students' cram course in civil rights was over. Everyone from the church gathered at the Ben Moore Hotel and we from SNCC discussed the events of the last three days. The lessons had been numerous. We regretted the serious difficulties we had had with members of SCLC and especially with Brother Bevel; we knew, however, that often in moments when tension is high, nerves are frayed, sleep is lost, and the enemy is out there, such things will occur. Especially when basic political differences lie beneath the surface.

Saturday night, March 13, a number of us in SNCC went to Selma and met to discuss future action and assignments. On Sunday, John Lewis and I went to New York to participate in a Harlem march of many thousands protesting events in Alabama. This was part of the nationwide protest for which we had issued a call. Our network of Friends of SNCC and other supporters in the U.S. and Canada had mounted numerous demonstrations at federal establishments. In Boston, students demonstrated at the U.S. Attorney General's office; in Los Angeles, students blocked mail trucks; in New York, the SNCC office organized a series of demonstrations at the federal courthouse. In Washington, students from Howard University sat-in at the White House itself. So continuous was the pressure there that President Johnson complained to H. Rap Brown and other SNCC representatives at a meeting of "civil-rights leaders" that his daughter Luci couldn't study.

On Monday, we returned to Montgomery and went immediately to the Alabama State University campus where the students were having a meeting. They planned to march that day. The chaplain and the university's director of public relations told them that if they marched, they would spoil King's plan for Alabama—the same plan of which Bevel had spoken earlier. I felt then, as on other occasions, that to a certain extent people exploited the authority of Dr. King for their own ends. Asked to speak, I said I would not discuss the SCLC position but that the students had the right to make up their own minds about participating. They decided to go.

Later, when we had begun marching toward the Capitol, these same students—at least four to five hundred of them—demonstrated a remarkable radicalization of attitude. We had reached the corner of High Street and Jackson Street, which is in the heart of the Negro neighborhood. The police stopped us. The entire Alabama State College administration, save the president, appeared and sought to persuade the students to return. The students shouted them down. The administration then tried to use some of the student leaders to achieve its purpose by having them call for a return to the campus and a meeting. The student leaders were also shouted down. Meanwhile, black residents had come out on their porches and were shouting to the students, "Don't you all go back!" The administration then asked me to use my influence. "No," I said, "because that's what's wrong with the whole country right now. You pick the Negro 'leader' and try to get him to use his influence. Present your position to the students yourselves." The administration representatives turned and left.

We were trapped at High and Jackson from about 2:30 until 6:30 P.M., when the police lines faded away. We moved forward then, about seven or eight blocks toward the Capitol, and were again entrapped—this time by state troopers as well as city police. While there, we heard that there was trouble back at High and Jackson; later, we learned that the county posse had charged into the area beating people, even charging up on the porches of homes to hit and smash. Some residents had thrown rocks, bricks, and bottles back at them. I spoke to one woman who showed me where a cracker on horseback had come up on her porch and broken her window as well as a glass door. The press reported that an ambulance on duty had come into the area at that point and been blocked by the residents. This story was widely accepted. Because of its viciousness, we took the unusual step of investigating a press report and learned that it had originated with UPI (United Press International). The Associated Press had refused to carry the story because, on checking, they found that in fact the ambulance had not been blocked but was simply parked. Brother Bevel, however, gave an AP interview in which he called the whole demonstration, and especially the blocking of the ambulance, irresponsible.

While the people at High and Jackson were being beaten, we had remained encircled a few blocks away. Someone had a transistor radio, and we listened. The voice of President Johnson came on the air. He was addressing a special night session of Congress with an announcement of the 1965 Voting Rights Bill which would go to the Congress two days later. There we stood, trapped in the darkness by the police, and heard Johnson say "We shall overcome." The nation was deeply moved; even Dr. King reportedly said that he cried when Johnson uttered those words. To us, they were tinkling, empty symbols.

Johnson also spoiled a good song that day, for to sing "We Shall Overcome" after that speech was to reawaken the sense of hypocrisy created by his use of the three words. The Administration knew that, by introducing strong legislation, it could curb the protest which had been mounting throughout the country—protest which, if continued, would have carried people on to other issues. In a similar way, the Selma-to-Montgomery march, which was due to start the following Sunday, served to kill off protest. I had felt this was true of the 1963 March on Washington. The Alabama march convinced me that these large, formalized events tend to give the participants a feeling that a victory has been accomplished when nothing has actually been changed and to diminish momentum when pressure should be sustained, intensified.

The next day, Tuesday, March 16, we decided to try and picket the Capitol again. That day became, for me, the last time I wanted to participate in a nonviolent demonstration. Many college students were there as well as local high-school students brought in by Willie Ricks of SNCC. Hundreds of Northern sympathizers also joined us. Sammy Younge and others had been active in getting students to come over from Tuskegee for this and all the other demonstrations of that week. There were over a thousand people altogether as we started out.

A small group of us crossed the street ahead of the others. Looking back, we saw the city police lined up in front of the larger group and assumed—fools that we were— that they stood there to protect the group. Suddenly the county posse charged into our small group on horseback:

hoofs trampling, the cops whopping people not with the usual billy clubs but with long sticks. One of them was swinging a lariat at me. Some of the people wanted to stand together; that would clearly be suicide, so we scattered. The city police would not let me back through the line to join the larger group. I could not help but feel that I was a particular target of the moment.

Later, the city police dispersed the larger group. My ability to continue engaging in nonviolent direct action snapped that day and my anger at the executive branch of the federal government intensified.

Shortly after the brutal police action, we received a request to meet with Dr. King and Ralph Abernathy. I was anxious to rejoin the demonstrators and assess our position, but the SCLC group—with whom we did meet out of deference—wanted to discuss the old question of relations with the ministers. King brought to the meeting several officials from the First Baptist Church and the Dexter Avenue Baptist Church to smooth things over. Actually, SNCC had already solved the church problem the day before: a small church on High Street had opened its doors to us and we used it as a base. Now the others agreed to cooperate, and we scheduled a mass meeting for that evening. We also decided that there would be a march to the County Courthouse the next day, led by Dr. King.

It was at the mass meeting that I uttered the words, "If we can't sit at the table of democracy, then we'll knock the fucking legs off." This statement was widely reported, usually accompanied by the report that there were some nuns in the church. The press, true to form, did not mention that I had added, "But before we tear it completely down, they will move to build a better one rather than see this one destroyed." At the time, I was immediately embarrassed by what I had said because many black women and

young children were present; I muttered words to that effect. The charge by the posse earlier that day, perhaps the
most brutal thing I had ever seen, was still in my mind. It
was difficult not to speak out in anger.

The next day, people marched to the courthouse and
stood in the rain for three solid hours. Inside, a group of
SNCC and SCLC people, as well as several ministers and
Montgomery bigwigs, plus representatives of the Federal
Community Relations Service, were negotiating with the
county sheriff. He agreed to issue a public apology for the
posse's charge. The others considered this a victory; we
found it a shallow triumph and continued demonstrating
until the end of the week when the march from Selma
finally began. The students' cram course in civil rights
was over.

VII The Toilet Revolution: Aftermath

The most important thing about the events in Montgomery, from my viewpoint, was their effect on the consciousness and commitment of the Tuskegee students. There had been three critical moments during the week of March 10–17: when the students had to decide whether or not to march despite Dr. King's ban, when they had to decide whether or not to stay at the Capitol on the first night, and when, on the following day, they had to choose to remain in the church or return to Tuskegee. Heated debate about the wisdom of the decisions took place in Montgomery and also back at Tuskegee, as the demonstrators returned from the state capital. Various people told me their opinions of the whole experience, step by step, beginning with the decision to march. One of them was Gwen Patton, who emerged from these events as a new student leader. Another was Maggie Magee, a teacher at Tuskegee Institute.

GWEN PATTON: I think the most important thing the students experienced was the fact that King, "the Lord," didn't tell them when they should move. That was a defiance right there within the civil-rights struggle. "The Lord" had told us we should move next week, and not this week. And the students said, "No, we're going to move this week. We're going to move now." And they were ready.

We got up that morning at about five-thirty to get on the buses. Everybody had little sandwiches, little lunch bags, that the cafeteria had fixed. We each had an apple and a bologna sandwich; we were going on a picnic. We grouped in twos; every guy had a girl. And we sat on the bus and sang freedom songs all the way down. We had no concept that we were going to meet state troopers and city police and be kicked out of that church. Nobody had that kind of idea. We were going to a very dignified thing that Tuskegee students had created all of their own.

When we left the First Baptist Church, going toward Dexter Avenue, it was still a rally. Then the shit really hit the fan when they found out that Governor Wallace wasn't coming out to speak to Tuskegee students, that they were no different from other black people—the county people, the people of Selma, anywhere. So the whole picnic idea was killed and people started being real, being honest with themselves.

TIAL had not organized. They couldn't build a viable organization because they themselves had not organized. We didn't even understand strategy; we didn't know what we were doing. But we were reacting to something that was happening inside of us, something that had to happen before we could even start talking to students outside. We had to get ourselves together.

MAGGIE MAGEE: One thing I learned is that you don't hold a meeting in the middle of a demonstration. That's what we tried to do in the streets of Montgomery when the question first came up about staying at the Capitol. That's when the group split.

I think we were still hung up on the idea that we've got to vote and we've got to discuss, because that's the only way TIAL had ever moved before. You've got to let everybody talk. And I don't know what would have happened if, in the middle of that street discussion about whether or not we should stay, the police had decided to move.

I remember when we were on the street and Jim Forman said, "If you're staying, sit down; if you're not, get out of here." And we sat down because we couldn't think of what else to do. That kind of choice came up quickly. Student leadership broke down. We were in the hands of SNCC. Things like the cameras—SNCC people said, "Don't look—they just want your picture." I would definitely say that we were held together that day and night by SNCC.

The time I was most frightened was when the police were getting ready to charge up and somebody said, "Men on the outside." Each thing you got through, you felt, "Well, I got through that. I've gained something." You felt that you couldn't break down.

All the students who went to Montgomery felt they had been through something. However, the students who stayed for the night felt they had been through more than that. You could almost make an equation: the longer you stayed in Montgomery, the more intense you became about the Movement.

LAURA PAYTON: I came back to the campus, and it seemed like I was different. People were saying to me, "Girl, you must be crazy. Why did you stay all night? We worried about you." So I said I didn't feel like anything was going to happen to me. I felt that I had to stay there, and I did. I can't explain what I mean by different, except that now I was so deeply involved in what is called the Movement.

My mother said, "We just knew you had gone down there to demonstrate." I told her that I did go. She said, "Well, I know you're not going to go back down there. You could get hurt." So I said, "I could get hurt crossing the street every day."

The attitude of one girl, who had not gone on the march at all, was significantly changed by the fact that others not only went but also stayed the night.

RUBY TAYLOR: I hadn't gone on the march. I have this personal thing about my folks because they'll be fired if their daughter or son gets involved in civil rights. My mother is a science teacher employed by the Pickens County School Board of Education. But that night, people came back to Tuskegee from Montgomery to get food and blankets and more people. Somebody got up at a meeting we had in the gym and said, "Well, they aren't going to let us in through the lines, so what are we going to do? Are we going to force our way in? If we force our way in, they're going to put us in jail." Eldridge Burns was talking about this fellow who didn't have but half a kidney, and he was sitting down there in the street, and what were we healthy people going to do? Were we going to sit there on campus as we usually do all week, or were we going to go in there? We were undecided. But I made up my mind that on the next march I would be there.

Among those who had gone and stayed in the church overnight, a new decision had to be made in the morning.

MAGGIE MAGEE: The spirit was good that night in the church. I remember I was very glad to see SNCC and the duffel bags. When the ministers came in and said, "Girls upstairs," people just howled. But the next morning, you could see how tired and dirty and hungry you were. SNCC had held us together that night, but the next morning I just didn't want to be held together anymore. My loyalty then was to TIAL. I wasn't sure what the objectives were any more—I just wanted to get out of there. So I left when the buses left. For me personally, things happened too fast. Now, looking back, I would argue that we should have stayed at the Capitol when it began to rain! But it took me six months to see that.

George Ware was another student who went back to Tuskegee after the night in the church, when the TIAL executive committee decided that people should leave.

GEORGE WARE: Things were in utter chaos at Tuskegee. The people who had gone back the day before, when we were at the Capitol, had apparently begun to feel very bad about leaving. The way they reacted was to say that nobody had told them about the dangers, which was a lie; that nobody had made any provisions for their protection, which was impossible and which they had known before they left. They developed all kinds of rationalizations about why the situation should never have developed in the first place.

The administration was saying that they had to quiet the whole thing down 'cause it had got totally out of hand. It was disrupting the campus community. Dean Phillips, who viewed himself as a liaison between TIAL and the administration, began to say that it had been a mistake for us to stay down there overnight, that we had to not only cool things on the campus but try to get people to come back from Montgomery. I was very confused as to just how I could go about doing that; I had already tried earlier that morning. Besides, I was ready to go to bed for twenty hours.

For two or three days, I was out of the whole argument because I was about to be suspended from the graduate program. My major professor had told me that if I went to Montgomery, he would drop me from the program. So I got embroiled in a discussion with the graduate school and had to gather materials to fight that.

Students kept coming back from Montgomery and we were holding continuous meetings, meetings which lasted twelve hours. In the middle of the night, students would come back, beaten up all over the head and saying that we just had to go back to Montgomery. We would have two to three hundred in the auditorium, talking about things. Wendy, Gwen, Simuel—that whole group got arrested and had to be bailed out. TIAL caught hell from both sides. There were the students who had left us down there originally saying, "Y'all were trying to get us killed," and then there were the students who stayed, saying, "Y'all are a bunch of Uncle Toms. You left us down there, and this is what happened."

There was beginning to be a lot of anti-TIAL and anti-SNCC feeling on that campus, and it was encouraged by the administration. In classrooms, instructors would say that TIAL was being manipulated by SNCC; that we never would have got involved in that mess if SNCC hadn't been there; that students should be very wary, first of SNCC and second of that little radical core in TIAL.

Clearly, SNCC sought to radicalize the Tuskegee students and to catalyze the emergence of a strong, militant leadership group. But SNCC did not deceive the students, nor force them in devious ways to make their decisions. The charge of manipulation usually came from those who feared militancy and radicalization. Others, like Jimmy Rogers—a Tuskegee student and Air Force veteran—took away a different impression of SNCC.

JIMMY ROGERS: I remember a SNCC worker, Annie Pearl Avery. During one demonstration, a policeman raised his stick and she reached up and snatched it out of his hand and threw it to the ground. She said, "What are you gonna do with that?" He stood there, and he was embarrassed. This was my first contact with the Student Nonviolent Coordinating Committee itself. My impression was sort of twofold. I said they're either bold or fools—or maybe crazy. I didn't know. It seemed like instead of the police intimidating them, they were intimidating the policemen. I couldn't understand this, coming from New York. I had heard how vicious the police in the South were and then I found out that they really were vicious but that all the Negroes in the South were not afraid of them. I feel that this was a part of growth, to see people react to brutality.

The division of opinion about SNCC actually reflected deeper divisions among the students.

GWEN PATTON: The people in TIAL were on different levels of militancy and on different intellectual levels. George Ware was highly intellectual and he could perceive far better than most of us. But then there were others who wanted results and didn't have time to theorize about what was going to happen. At the church, the students were given the strategy question. To stay in that church would have been a defiance of TIAL. It became a problem of being a group or an individual. We hadn't matured enough to really discuss that. We didn't have any degree of flexibility. It was a plan—you did *A*, you did *B*, you did *C*, but if *C* didn't work out right then you didn't know what to do.

But there was an awakening of militancy that I'd never seen before. There were maybe sixty people really willing to lay their lives on the line. The problem was, they couldn't understand why the others hadn't reached the same level. They became impatient with their fellow students. Out of that grew conflict, and I hate to say it but I think I was one of the main persons always creating conflict. Still, that day at the church was the day TIAL really got organized.

JIMMY ROGERS: That march brought TIAL closer together, that's true. But TIAL didn't leave the door open, didn't encourage other people to come in. And people played up the Montgomery thing—"I've been to jail in Montgomery three times." "Well, I've been to jail in Montgomery five times." "But I also went to jail in Selma." This is what people were saying to each other instead of really helping their brothers along.

GWEN PATTON: I don't think people were trying to prove a point to the others, they were trying to prove a point within themselves—that it's not important for me to go to class every day to learn sociology when I've been hoofed by a horse in Montgomery. What alienated people from TIAL was that some students had stopped caring about that which seemed so important to the others. After the march, a lot of people couldn't take Tuskegee any more. They had come to a realization within themselves; they had seen what their education was doing to them. But some of them weren't strong enough to deal with it—defying their parents, defying the school, defying the whole society.

There were bad repercussions from that march, and

there were good ones. The most important thing was that it gave people like Simuel Schutz a direction. We developed a lot of people out of it.

The Montgomery experience provided the students with few answers, but it did make them focus on important questions: What are my present goals as a black student? Is it enough for me just to get an education so that I can join (or remain in) the professional middle class? Does the administration of my school stand for progress or the status quo? Where do I stand in relation to that administration? What is the function of a student organization, and how do I relate to it? How far am I willing to go in order to end the oppression of black people? Who—to put it most basically—am I, and what is the meaning of my life as a black person in white America?

But, as Gwen Patton said, Montgomery had one very tangible effect. Out of the week's events emerged a hard-core group of student leaders who were ready to put their lives on the line. Montgomery was important primarily because it produced a nucleus of militants who continued to be active and who, in several cases, are still active today. This nucleus included some Tuskegee students who later became full-time SNCC workers: Jimmy Rogers, Jennifer Lawson, George Ware, Simuel Schutz. Then there were those who continued as Tuskegee students but spent more time in the Movement than in the classroom, among them Gwen Patton, Wendy Paris, Warren Hamilton—and Sammy Younge, Jr.

Sammy had been among those who stayed at the Capitol on the first day. With only one imperfectly functioning kidney, and remembering the doctor's warning to avoid catching cold, he nonetheless remained out there on the pavement in the chilly March night. Knowing that a blow to his side could be fatal, he had nonetheless stayed out there on the street where the cops could do anything they wanted at any time. Thus, he made his first major decision about life-and-death values.

At that time, I did not know about Sammy's physical condition. In the early part of the day, he was an amorphous personage to me. He and Wendy Paris were serving informally as guards on the march. They came up to me and we talked. His face and his conduct left an impression. I saw his reactions to the ministers when they tried to take over the march and run things. I remember talking with him after we got back to the church at two in the morning. I liked his reactions.

The next day, I wasn't sure where he stood. On the one hand, I felt that his sympathies were with the coalition that wanted to stay. On the other hand, he was very imbued with the spirit of Tuskegee—the idea that the students had to act as a group. More than once, he came to me explaining that he was going to stay, he'd be right there. Later, when the bus was loading to go back, he came up and said, "Well, look, little brother, I'm going to go back. I'm going to try to get students on the campus to come back here because we have to have a unified student body."

For a minute I thought, "Well, you too." But I said, "Okay, man." Because I felt that what the students were going through was a learning experience and people had to find out that the concept of unity was impossible in a student body as large and diverse as Tuskegee. I also understood the conflict and turmoil in the students, all of whom had come unprepared and were now tired, hungry, dirty, wondering what their parents were thinking, what the school was thinking. Sammy's decision to go back seemed very reasonable in terms of the overall situation. I found him that day to be a person who always understood what was going on, what issues were involved, regardless of what he himself did. He also stood out among the students that day for his work in the background—moving around, talking to people.

Sammy had told me that he would be back in Montgomery, and he did come back—to transport people, and to maintain communications. He witnessed some of the worst brutality, including the charge by the county posse. It is hard to be sure of what Sammy was thinking in those days, but the comments of old friends and SNCC workers suggest his newborn commitment as well as his awareness of the danger of physical injury to himself. He resolved the conflict between these two forces by choosing certain forms of participation.

LALY WASHINGTON: I wasn't there, but Sammy told me how people couldn't go to the bathroom and all that. He was very concerned about keeping people there that first night and got frustrated because they weren't cooperating.

ELDRIDGE BURNS: The first time when we took the whole group down to Montgomery, Sammy really dug that. Then, when some of us decided to go to Montgomery to demonstrate again, he stayed in Tuskegee. We went to jail. When we came back, we had a little conference that night and Sammy was there. He felt sort of bad about everybody going to jail and him not going. He thought that people would hold it against him because certain guys thought that going to jail was a big thing. But he was really afraid of it. People just didn't know how afraid Sammy was about going to jail.

BILL HALL: A lot of things were going on, and they gave the students an opportunity to participate on different levels —not only in demonstrations, but in making decisions and in trying to get other students to join the demonstrations. That's when we really got involved with Sammy. SNCC set up a student conference for a weekend, from Friday through Sunday. They were still demonstrating in Montgomery, and it was very important that the demonstrations continue, but it was also important that the conference be held. Sammy was one of the few students who elected to stay and help with that conference.

WENDY PARIS: I guess you could say that Eldridge and Sammy involved me. Sammy had started going to meetings and he told me, "Come on over there, man, it's a pretty good thing. You ain't doing nothing no way." So I went on over there, and I got involved. And we worked together.

WILLIE RICKS: Sometimes you baptize people, and they don't even know they're being baptized. We in SNCC knew that only five or ten out of hundreds of people in Montgomery would be willing to do some work, to take it beyond the marches. Sammy happened to be one of the people who decided he would carry it way beyond that.

A young teacher at Tuskegee, who later became a full-time SNCC worker, recalled the emergence of Sammy as a leader.

JEAN WILEY: At first, Sammy was just another one of the several hundred students who went to Montgomery. When I returned to Tuskegee, I was told that a student had stood before a group the night before and had begun to talk about the very pressing racial questions in Alabama. He defined the student role as he saw it. Most of the people were faculty members and they were *very* impressed with this kid, as they called him. From the time that he returned to Montgomery, Sammy became one of the major students in civil rights on the campus. He started organizing students, became one of the major people in TIAL.

Sammy also began working closely with SNCC. At that time (and still today) the organization had no formal membership, only a staff of full-time workers. But there were many people, like Sammy Younge, who did not serve full-time and yet were considered SNCC people. "A band of brothers, a circle of trust," we sometimes called ourselves. One of the symbols of that broad membership was a style of dress which characterized our workers at that time and represented our commitment to the black people of the abandoned, impoverished rural South.

GEORGE WARE: It was a complete transformation. At first, Sammy had come down to Montgomery in his Ivy League jacket and a tie. Then he would be wearing dungarees with the jacket. Then he got a denim jacket.

ELDRIDGE BURNS: Later on, he went down and bought himself a pair of overalls and a pea-coat and an old two-dollar hat that would sit up real high—one of those trainman's caps. He had some old boots from the Navy. And he would say, "Well, man, I'm ready now. Let's go, doctor." So we went to a meeting.

Another person who recalled the transformation was Stokely Carmichael, then working in Lowndes County, Alabama—about fifty miles from Tuskegee. On the night that the Selma-to-Montgomery march ended, Mrs. Viola Liuzzo of Detroit was murdered by Klansmen in Lowndes. She had been transporting marchers to their homes. SNCC immediately sent in workers to organize people for voter registration and political action; within a week of Mrs. Liuzzo's death, the first mass meeting took place. Not one of the blacks who constitute eighty per cent of Lowndes' population was registered at that time. In less than a year, they would be forming an independent, local political party—independent because in Alabama the Democratic Party meant George Wallace and an emblem showing a white rooster with the motto "White Supremacy . . . for the right." They would also bring an end to the rule of terror in Lowndes, by making it clear that black people were no longer going to sit back and be shot down like dogs. They would fight back, if attacked.

The name of the new, independent party was the Lowndes County Freedom Organization, its emblem a black panther. Carmichael headed the SNCC project in Lowndes. He had originally met Sammy Younge in Washington, and Sammy went over to visit the Lowndes workers several times.

STOKELY CARMICHAEL: Sammy had been a big man on campus, a good-looking cat, and he always dressed well. Had his own car. When he started working with SNCC, he wore his dungarees on campus and everybody began to draw back from him. He was isolated—you know, the same shit everybody goes through on the Negro college campuses. Then he made a complete break. He told them, fuck it, he was going with SNCC. He went SNCC and he just had nothing to do with those folks.

Sammy Younge, child of the middle class, went "Snick" in all the big and little ways of the organization.

ELDRIDGE BURNS: One night, we were on the phone calling people in the North to donate money for bail and things. Sammy had a list of all these names and he was calling people at about four o'clock in the morning and saying, "This is the Student, uh, Student Violent Coordinating Committee."

VIII   On the Move

During the remaining months of his first semester at Tuskegee Institute, Sammy Younge lived and breathed "the Movement" while continuing to search for his own direction within it. About three weeks after the Selma-Montgomery march ended, he left Alabama and headed over to a long-time SNCC battlefield in the state of Mississippi. This was Sunflower County: birthplace of the White Citizens' Council (the rich man's KKK), domain of plantation-owner Senator James Eastland, home of 31,000 poor and oppressed black citizens. Mrs. Fannie Lou Hamer, a Sunflower resident and a leader of the Mississippi Freedom Democratic Party (MFDP), had called on us for more people to work on a voter-registration campaign geared to the municipal elections scheduled for May 11. Sammy Younge, along with about seven other students, went to help during their Easter vacation in late April.

Sammy and a young lady named Jolien Hightower transported people from Ruleville, where Mrs. Hamer lived, to register at the county seat, and back again. From the time he arrived, Sammy was turned on by this new experience. He learned, among other things, about some of the local methods used to maintain white supremacy and keep down the black population—including the notorious practice of performing hysterectomies on unsuspecting black women who come to the hospital for other purposes.

JEAN WILEY: Two nights after he left for Mississippi, Sammy called and asked me to tell Dean Phillips and all of his teachers that he would be there a week longer than expected. He also told me that they had been chased by

117

some white people that day. I got very upset and asked him to please be careful, but I felt it was useless.

WENDY PARIS: We talked to Mrs. Hamer of Ruleville and she psyched us. She brought a truth to the light. I saw something they called a hospital where they had a dentist as a surgeon. They nicknamed that place "the slaughter pen" because sixty per cent of the Negro women who go in there come back infertile. They sterilize them. We talked to a fifteen-year-old Negro girl who had been in there and who couldn't have any more children. Now she was working on voter registration with us, coming around every day.

After we left, we were going to get us a pretty little car and go back someday. The people down there kind of liked us. They were piecing a quilt to give us when we came back. Sammy wanted to go back real soon, but we told him we needed to work in Tuskegee. We argued, oh man, about ten days. "Well, do what you want, Sam, but I thought we wanted to work in Tuskegee, man. I thought that we wanted to bring light around Tuskegee." We finally got him to stay here.

GWEN PATTON: He was very impressed by the Mississippi experience. When Sammy got back, he talked to me for two hours about the MFDP and Mrs. Hamer. He didn't think an Alabama Freedom Democratic Party could work because we didn't have basically the same type of people here as in Mississippi. The whole state of Mississippi was in constant oppression but in Alabama you could have a Montgomery or a Tuskegee, where a lot of black people lived without feeling so consciously oppressed all the time.

RUBY TAYLOR: After he went to Mississippi, we just knew

that Sammy was going to go crazy. He had got himself
really tied up in the Movement. He would talk with a little
hum in his voice at the end of a sentence, like a preacher.
I think maybe he picked that up from some of the SNCC
workers. Also, he had let his hair grow long.

The new hairstyle, like the new clothing before it,
was only a symbol, but it represented a changing consciousness in Sammy. One aspect may have been his attraction
to "revolutionary glamor"; SNCC affiliation had a romantic appeal based on our commitment to the poor and our
history of challenging racism in the most dangerous areas.
But I also think that Sammy had found in SNCC a group
of people whose purpose in life he considered real, unlike
the Tuskegee world with its concern for status and status
quo. He had found a community in which he could feel
comfortable.

For the older Negroes of Tuskegee, Sammy's haircut
was just one more reason to be upset about "that boy" and
his defiance of local mores. Even Laly Washington's
mother (sometimes called "Big Laly") criticized his appearance. But no one could stop Sammy or others of his
generation from rejecting middle-class standards and affirming their identity with blackness.

MRS. WASHINGTON: I said to him, "Why don't you cut
that nappy hair, you look awful. Go get your hair cut."
Sammy would tell me, "Gonna cut my hair when I get
my freedom." I'd say, "What kind of freedom is that, 'my
freedom'? Man, you'll need nets and hairpins and everything else before that time!"

I kidded him about his overalls, too, and told him that
I didn't see the point. What was he trying to prove? He

would say, "Well, you don't know when you're going to get arrested, and I can't go down there in my good suit." And I told him, "Well, at least you're clean."

LALY WASHINGTON: My mother thought it was just horrible. She pestered Sammy about getting a haircut, and he would say, "O.K., Big Laly. I'm going to get a haircut." Of course he never did. I had got an Afro when I was in Chicago working with CORE, and my hair was shorter than Sammy's. My mother wrote letters all the time asking me to let it grow. Finally I decided I would let it grow for when I went home, just to please her. Then, when I got back to Chicago, I would have it cut again. The haircut thing became a big issue in Tuskegee.

Sammy came back from Mississippi with a strong interest in working among rural people and in voter registration. He was still uncertain about exactly where he wanted to organize, and he continued to talk about returning to Mississippi. SNCC staffers in Tuskegee urged him to remain. But your own home town can be the hardest place in the world to organize, especially if it's a place like Tuskegee.

About seventeen miles away, in a rural area, there was a small town called Brownsville. Sammy had been casually visiting people there for a while; he felt freer in Brownsville, with its less pretentious people and way of life, than in his own home town. Now he could try out some of his ideas from Mississippi there. And so, although he was not yet sure about where he would work on a long-range basis, he decided to concentrate his efforts on Brownsville and voter registration for a while.

At that time, TIAL decided to divide its activities into

two areas—voter registration headed by Sammy and direct action under Gwen Patton. Sammy began to recruit students to work on organizing "the rural." Simultaneously, he began setting up the first Freedom Day ever held in Tuskegee.

The immediate basis for that event was an injunction recently issued by Judge Frank Johnson, the same judge with whom SCLC had negotiated about marching. This injunction outlawed certain questions in the old Alabama voter-registration test. The test, in use since 1964, had been challenged by a Justice Department suit in 1965 on the grounds that it was too difficult and discriminated against black people: it had one hundred possible variations of questions about the state government, the U.S. Constitution, etc. Now, however, people only had to answer some eight questions such as name, address, and so forth. Plans to take advantage of the injunction were therefore made, and on a Monday in early May, Sammy went to Brownsville with a group of students to bring people into Tuskegee to register on this first Freedom Day. Among those working with him in Brownsville were students like George Ware and "Red" Robinson, and SNCC field secretary Bill Hall.

GEORGE WARE: We selected Brownsville because people there knew Sammy and because most of the Negroes there owned their own land. We figured that if those people could start a whole thrust for being registered to vote, we might get enough registered to challenge that black middle class in town.

BILL HALL: We took four people, just four people, back into Tuskegee to register that first time. Those four were very significant to Sammy because he really wanted to work in voter registration and he looked upon it with great pride. It was good from the community's viewpoint, too, because Sammy was doing something in Brownsville that had not been done—a person from Tuskegee going out there and actively showing his concern. He had already been going up to Brownsville on his own, but after the Freedom Day, a group of us began going up every week for political education and discussion.

"RED" ROBINSON: It started off with one man and one lady about seventy or eighty years of age. The man was an old deacon in the church, and through him Sammy got approval from the deacons to use the church in Brownsville for meetings.

BILL HALL: They voted to let Sammy use the church on, I believe, Friday evenings. This was important because there was an educational program which ran up to 8:00 P.M. in the school next door to the church. Our program began at eight, which meant that people could just come from the school into the church.

"RED" ROBINSON: You should have seen the light in Sammy's eyes and everybody else's eyes when we went out there for that first, organized meeting. You can't talk about large numbers because there were only twenty or twenty-five, but people were really interested. We sang a few freedom songs and then we went into the use of the application blank, the why and the importance. The people would come and sit and really work on this form—you know, how to fill it out.

ELDRIDGE BURNS: Sammy really got excited about taking the people to register. He liked to say "reddish," the way

people talk: "I'm going to take those people to 'reddish.'"
And the people out in Brownsville really liked Sammy.
One day he went and helped them plow and move stumps
—you know, those big stumps in the field. He must have
plowed for about three days.

"RED" ROBINSON: After about a month and a half, Sammy
had the Brownsville community so set that if Sammy
wasn't there to carry on a meeting, some of the people in
that community would carry on their own meeting. Bill
Hall suggested to Sammy that he should leave Brownsville
because these people had to go all the way for themselves,
but to come back every now and then and watch. So
Sammy decided to go into other communities and organize
them as he had Brownsville.

ANN PRATT: Sammy took me with him to Linette and
Alexander City and a lot of other places. We drove all day
long. He was trying to find this one minister. We went all
over town looking for the guy. I said, "Sammy, I don't
think we're going to find him—not today, anyway." He
said, "Oh yeah, we'll find him." We went to this place
and that place, and finally we did find the man.

Sammy would talk to a lot of people. These were
strangers, and right away he'd sort of establish something
with the person. We went to the high school in Linette
and talked to one of the teachers. She sat down in the
lunchroom and she talked to Sammy and me for about an
hour.

Along with the success he experienced, Sammy
Younge learned some lessons about organizing and had
some of the organizer's common problems.

GEORGE WARE: At first, we had a whole romantic concept of "local people" out in the county, about how they would perceive TCA and the black middle class generally. We thought that we could go out there and talk to them about the fact that the black middle class was not interested in solving their problems and that it would be a real snap. We found out that you couldn't really talk too negatively about Tuskegee or any of that middle class to those people out in the county because TCA is old, and there's a lot of respect for it. They haven't done anything for the county people but they always have someone going out there and talking. Also, the people look and say, "Yeah, those folks really know what they are doing. They live just like white folks."

Sammy was the first person to start saying that when you go out there, avoid criticizing. Raise another issue. Just talk about the people's problems and avoid criticizing the black middle class, 'cause you alienate a lot of those people if you start out like that.

ELDRIDGE BURNS: Sometimes Sammy and Wendy worked with Simuel Schutz—people called him Junior. One night, at a mass meeting Sammy had organized, Junior got disgusted because people were arguing. They weren't ready to move just yet. Junior cursed them out, and then Sammy got mad with him and everything. "Man, I'm through. I'm through. I'm through," he said. The next day he'd taken off his jeans. But then stuff began getting back into him, and he started right over again.

Another time he got discouraged, but all he needed was somebody to push him a little bit. Winky [Bill Hall], in a meeting, committed Sammy. He said, "Sammy's the only one that's doing something." And when he said that, Sammy was gone again.

Sammy's concern for the problems of the rural people extended beyond voter registration. One of his other projects involved the federal program which provided the poor with vitally needed surplus food supplies. This program, financed by Washington but administered locally, has often been used in the South as a weapon against black people.

GWEN PATTON: There was some surplus food that was to come into Macon County. The City Council, for some reason, didn't want the food to come—they felt it would conflict with the Tuskegee image and it would expose the poverty of the county, if they just gave things away. So they voted not to have it. Sammy talked before the City Council, argued, talked with the welfare people. Finally they voted to have the surplus food brought into Macon County.

Another time Sammy became very involved with county people was over low-rent housing. They have low-rent housing in Macon County for white people and they also have it for black people. The man in charge is a black man on campus, Dr. T. S. Williams, who is now a City Councilman. Sammy knew some people who needed to move into a low-rent housing unit. He got the application for them and found out there were vacancies in the white unit. Williams told them there were no houses. Sammy fought and fought. I don't think the people ever got that unit, but Sammy did raise some very basic questions that upset a lot of people in the community. Sammy dealt with real issues. He didn't just demonstrate and picket.

Sammy and the other TIAL students worked occasionally to desegregate public accommodations. The word "desegregate" as opposed to "integrate" is important. For the TIAL militants, integration had no great meaning or value—especially in Tuskegee where the facilities for black people were often superior to those for whites. But attempts to desegregate were a way of challenging racism in supposedly interracial Tuskegee. They were a way of exposing the lie of "the model town."

At that time, civil-rights workers often went out to "test" public accommodations for compliance with the 1964 Civil Rights Act. A common way to do this was by having a group of black people try to get in. If they were refused, a group of whites would then enter and obtain proof that they had been served. Such proof would then be turned over to an attorney for a suit to be brought against the establishment.

GWEN PATTON: Pat's Café up in Lakeview was Sammy's idea. Sammy and Wendy knew this town backward and forward. They knew every white man that owned anything in Tuskegee by his first name, and they called them by their first names. Sammy was sort of frightened of going up to Lakeview because Lakeview is a truck stop on Route 80, and he didn't like the threat of guns. But we went to Pat's Café and we pushed this little bell. They wouldn't let us in and said it was a private club. Sammy said we ought to get Maggie, Tom, and that exchange student from St. Olaf's—they were white—to go to that café and get in, get a receipt, and bring it back to prove that it wasn't a private club. So they did.

Another of Sammy's targets that spring was job discrimination in Tuskegee proper.

GWEN PATTON: Sammy had this great idea one day to go and investigate the stores downtown. Sammy and I and Jimmy Rogers went downtown to the different merchants and asked about hiring policies. We put in our applications for jobs. We got a negative response from every store in town except the Big Bear, I think.

Then we went to the A&P where they employed no Negroes except a man who had been pushing carts and carrying groceries outdoors for about fifteen years. We asked to see the manager. This guy said he wasn't there, but we believed he was there. We asked if they had any jobs available. He didn't say anything to that. We asked him what were they paying their workers, and he didn't answer that either. We explained that we were interested in jobs for the summer to help pay for going back to school in September and that we wanted application forms. He refused to give them to us. We decided then that we would boycott the A&P.

Sammy, who had not even thought about it much, was the main one to do the mediating on this. He was the one who discussed the ultimatum and so forth. We started picketing in early May. We had student support at that time, and we would picket all day long until the store closed. Sammy helped organize different picket lines—how they were supposed to picket every hour or every two hours and the like.

GEORGE WARE: After two days of the boycott, this cat's business fell something like ninety per cent, 'cause most of the people who usually went in there were black people. But we were very naïve. We didn't have any concept of the strategy that people can employ to freeze you out. We had this cat over the barrel, and he said he would hire Negroes if we gave him a certain period of time. We agreed. So he went over to the A&P in Auburn where they had a Negro already working and brought that man over to work here. By then, our ability to mobilize people around the issue had been lost.

The A&P picketing resulted in Sammy's being insulted and threatened; at one point, a white man drew a switch-blade knife on him and SNCC worker Jimmy Rogers. It also brought about a strong reaction from some of the middle-class black residents. What had begun as just another project soon burgeoned into widespread controversy.

RUBY TAYLOR:　On the way home from picketing, we were walking past this white high school. Most of us had dark skin, and Sammy looked like a white fellow walking along there beside me. White kids came by and called him "nigger lover," and that really got next to him. One of them even spit on him.

GEORGE WARE:　The A&P was our first major action in Tuskegee itself. We had always got a lot of support from the black people there as long as we were doings things like sending people to Mississippi to help Mrs. Hamer. But the minute we started attacking the A&P that town did a complete about-face. It showed in the way they viewed us, in our ability to raise money and to function.

GWEN PATTON:　The pressure in the community became so great that there was talk about "deporting" all the young people in TIAL out of Tuskegee. One night they had a mass meeting in Logan Hall. Sammy's mother came to see TIAL in action, to see if what the people in the community had been saying was true. She sat there and listened, and she was very proud of her son.

This project to deport them was spearheaded by one of the "respectable citizens" of the community, Leroi Johnson. He felt they were messing up this model community and making it hard for people like him and the liberals.

The A&P picketing brought the TIAL activists face-to-face with community attitudes. To the middle-class Negroes, people like Sammy were just "wild," "irresponsible," dungaree-wearing "kids" who threatened to rock the Model Town boat. They were "irresponsible," of course, because they didn't fall into line with the local Establishment. Furthermore, the older people had known the youths from childhood, so they would gossip about family background or adolescent escapades and thus undermine the young people's organizing efforts.

Another label frequently put on the TIAL militants by their critics was that old familiar Red one. Sometimes the students dealt with this problem in a very imaginative way.

GWEN PATTON: One of the tricks that I can't forget, we pulled on Beulah Johnson. She used to call us communists. Sammy and I and others called up the FBI and told them that there was a person in the community who knew an awful lot about communists and we strongly suspected she might be one; maybe they should investigate her. The FBI did go to her house and talked to her. Later on, she called us up and hollered about how we put the FBI on her.

TIAL's relations with the Tuskegee Institute authorities also became abrasive at times, although they remained essentially good in this period.

GEORGE WARE: When most of the students had returned from Montgomery, the school wanted to make sure it would never happen again. So they had said that each person would have to send a form home to get permission from his parents to participate in the Movement, specifying where. The parents would thereby remove responsibility from the school; they called it *"en loco parentis"* [*sic*]. That meant that if you wanted to have a demonstration, it would take you damn near two weeks to figure out who could go where. We told Dean Phillips that we would study the proposal and then make a final decision. After looking at it and talking with Bill Hall, who said it was a crock of shit, we told Phillips, "Hell no. We're not going to accept it."

We began to talk about moving off campus. Sammy went down and got this place for about thirty dollars a month. We moved in typewriters and set up a TIAL office.

TIAL had its internal conflicts as well, and they dated back to the Montgomery demonstrations. The group identity thing was gone; the old leadership had faded; personality and power conflicts developed, sometimes between TIAL and SNCC people. When there was a hassle in TIAL, it tended to produce factions instead of compromise.

A number of TIAL activists were also torn by personal conflicts. They simply could not deal with the contradiction between Tuskegee Institute and the life for which it was preparing them, and the events which had taken place only thirty minutes away in Montgomery.

Tuskegee said: Get an education and you won't be a nigger. Montgomery had said: You're a nigger no matter what you do. Tuskegee said: Join our safe little middle class and forget what's outside. Montgomery had said: Black people are oppressed in this state, and you cannot turn your back on that. There was no connection between the campus classroom and what had happened in front of the State Capitol. Which was real? Under the pressure of trying to answer that question, four students had nervous breakdowns that spring. One of them was George Davis, whose organizing abilities and mind had made him an outstanding figure in TIAL. Even after he recovered he withdrew from the scene.

Meanwhile, Sammy went on working. Everyone agreed that he was the most active organizer in this difficult period. He still had not yet focused his energies; he was trying various forms of attack, probing various issues—voter registration, segregation, job discrimination. He wasn't even sure whether or not he wanted to remain and work in the Tuskegee area. But one thing had become clear: Sammy did not care much about school.

ELDRIDGE BURNS: He said, "Well, I got a course under Maggie Magee, and I got a course under Leslie Sherover, and they might give me two C's. I'm going to flunk math, though." That's all the credits he was taking. "Maybe, if I'm lucky, Leslie might give me a B. I can't fool Maggie, but I think Leslie sort of likes me." He had to write about thirty themes for Maggie that he hadn't done when he was supposed to, so everyone was going to write one for him. And they did, but he lost them someplace.

MAGGIE MAGEE: I had him in class from January 1965 to May 1965, in a course called "Special Communications."

What with all his civil-rights activities and everything, it was hard for Sammy to be in class. We met at one o'clock in the afternoon on Monday, Wednesday, and Friday, and for a long time, Sammy would be out in the street or at the gate of the Institute collecting money. Sometimes he had one meeting after another so when he came to class, he slept. Once he came with Willie Peacock and they had a meeting in the class. He just had other things to do, so he brought the other things with him.

When he had an assignment for class he would sort of mumble, "Maggie . . ." and "I don't have it done." Then he'd look up at me. Leslie and I used to say secretly that he could ask almost anything with his eyes and get it.

There was a dance once, and I thought it would be fun to go downtown and buy a SNCC jacket like Sammy's. I wore it, and he asked me to dance. I told him that there were some things I couldn't do. So he was teaching me how to do this dance and he would say, "You put the subject *here*, and you put the verb *there*, then *punctuate!*"

Sammy couldn't spell things like segregation and integration. I suppose he could spell them, but there were just too many other things on his mind rather than whether the *i* went before the *e* or not. He taught me, a white teacher, a lot of things about what a real hang-up my students have, trying to decide whether the *i* comes before the *e*, or going out and doing something about public facilities. And Sammy could talk. He would stand up there sometimes with a loudspeaker or in the ballroom of the Student Union and talk. When I heard him, I decided that he was a real course in communications all by himself.

Sammy's speaking style, people said, was like that of a Baptist preacher. He would talk in a voice that hummed

and cracked, perhaps repeating a phrase ten times, rocking
back and forth on the microphone with his eyes blazing.
Although his style became accentuated after his trip to
Mississippi, some friends remembered that he had spoken
that way before. His was never the "cultured" speaking
style of middle-class Tuskegee.

Another teacher described the strong effect of Sammy's personality, particularly on women.

JEAN WILEY: Many people talked about Sammy's eyes,
but I don't know that anybody has talked about Sammy's
smile. He had a very honest, almost naïve, gay smile.
His eyes, together with his smile, attracted people to him
and attracted women, girls, by the score. It seemed to say,
I sort of trust you. He would talk about problems, like
working out in the county, and then all of a sudden he
would look at you and smile. You just didn't know what
to do. You knew that he was a man and doing a man's job,
but on the other hand, you were afraid because that smile
meant that there was so much hope and dedication.

"Girls by the score" seems to have been literally true.
One of his old buddies, Eldridge Burns, ran it down.

ELDRIDGE BURNS: He had a thing about girls. If Sammy
didn't have a girl, just somebody to go by, see his "old
lady" as he called it, he couldn't make it. As long as I can
remember, everyone he met he was so in love with that
he had to marry them—that was his way. When we were
in Washington, there was this girl named Angela and he
was going to marry her. But then he came home and
saw Karen and he wasn't going to marry Angela any
more; he was going to marry Karen. Then he went into

the Navy and met a girl named Kathy. Kathy was going to come to Tuskegee, but the minute she was supposed to come he didn't love her anymore. He was in love with Rose; then he didn't love Rose anymore. He was in love with Burell and he was going to marry her; he used to come down from the Navy to see her. He came down one Homecoming weekend and she wasn't there. He met another girl, so he didn't love Burell anymore. Then there was Doris, and he thought he liked her. Then he fell in love with Mildred, and he was going to marry Mildred. Then he fell back in love with Karen, and he was going to marry Karen. Then he met Ann, and he was going to marry Ann. She understood him. She wouldn't bother him too much. But he wasn't sure. Then there was Jean. And he really bought Jean a ring. Then came the time and he took his ring back and we bought Christmas presents with the money down in Montgomery one night. Then he fell in love with Karen again, and Karen said, "Well, Sammy, if you'll ever be something—if you'd be a doctor—then, man, we could make it." So Sammy was going to be a doctor. Then he was going to be a lawyer, you know, political science and all. Then he didn't love Karen any more. Who else was there? Oh yeah, he was in love with Billy, and then he got tired of Billy because she was always talking about some other boy. But you know, Billy liked him. And then he liked Twinkle, but Twinkle's mother wouldn't let her go with him because she didn't trust him, so he quit Twinkle and then he met Ralphine. He didn't really like Ralphine at first, and I don't think Ralphine really liked him at first, but it was just a thing with them. Sammy had a goo-gob of girls up at Talladega, too. We used to go there every weekend. All the time, just when it came time for him to get married, he would call and say, "Girl, don't come down here now."

He always liked your girl, too. He used to write letters to a girl I was going with. The letters never made any sense. He used words from songs, like "I love you like the highest mountain" and "till every river runs dry" and all that kind of thing. When I found out, he'd say, "Well, man, I know I wrote your girl, but I didn't mean anything by it. I didn't think I was doing anything wrong, man. You understand, don't you?" I said, "Yeah, Lemon. I understand."

WENDY PARIS: He was something. He dropped one every day, and she would still say she loved him. We used to get on him all the time. "Sammy, you doing these women wrong. You messin' us up too."

To some people, Sammy seemed like a real Don Juan; others had a different image of his relations with girls.

LALY WASHINGTON: Sammy had always kind of been in love with Karen. He'd break up with Karen the minute she was away and then he would go with someone else. Then he would break up with that person and then it was Karen. He never went back to any other girl I can think of more than once, other than Karen.

BILL HALL: Jolien Hightower and Doris Wilson were the two most important women in his life, as far as I could tell. I think he felt happiest when he was dominated by a woman, when she gave him some kind of direction. But he was jealous too; he liked to be able to isolate a woman away from the competition. Karen was just too much for him. She wouldn't stay isolated.

GWEN PATTON: I've never known Sammy not to have a girlfriend, but it was different from other guys in the movement. It was an altogether different thing. For instance, Jolien became one of the most important women in his life. He had to be with Jolien. When he was going to Mississippi, Jolien had to go. There was a real closeness that he had with girls.

BILL HALL: That's 'cause he promised to marry them.

LALY WASHINGTON: With all his girls, Sammy never stopped lecturing me about guys. I was going with this guy who was also going with another girl. Sammy constantly reprimanded me, played big-time father with me. "I don't want you seeing Robert any more," he would say. We were like brother and sister. If anything was bothering me, he'd make sure that something got done about it. We argued and fussed and fought, but he always worried about me and we were real honest with each other.

ANN PRATT: I wasn't really Sammy's girl, you might say. I don't think you could describe our relationship as easily as that. Sammy used to say that I was good *for* him but I wasn't good *to* him. Maybe there is some truth in that because I was always yelling at him and telling him, "Sammy, don't do this," and "Sammy, don't do that." He'd say I yelled all the time, but he'd tell me, "Don't stop yelling." I guess he figured I yelled because I cared about him. And I did, an awful lot. He'd say, "Well, Pratt"—that's what he used to call me; he never called me by my first name— "Don't ever stop yelling at me."

Sammy was loud at times, but then again there were times when people, other people, didn't see him. These were the times that we'd sit down and talk and he was no longer rowdy. We'd talk about a lot of things, and he could be very tender at times, as opposed to the person you saw at the College Union.

He used to come over to the campus late at night and whistle at the window. He would get somebody to wake me up. Most of the time, he just wanted somebody to talk to. And I'd talk to him and yell at him and tell him to go on home, that it was getting late. "Okay, Pratt, I'll see you tomorrow." And the next day he would come around again saying, "What you gonna do, little momma? What you gonna do?" So I says, "Oh, Sammy, what are you up to?" "Come on. Let's take a ride." Let's do this or let's do that. He was always on the move.

Perhaps Sammy's relationships with girls are best understood within the context of his general search for direction. He would seek, then hold on to something for a while, then seek again. "Always on the move," as Ann Pratt said. Everyone who knew Sammy Younge commented on his impatience and restlessness.

JEAN WILEY: He didn't like long meetings. After an hour of talking strategy, he would pace the floor or decide to get a coke or something. I think that was because he had ideas of his own and he felt people ought to see them. When they didn't, he would go out and wait until people decided to do the thing that he had thought of in the first place.

WENDY PARIS: Everything was always hurry, hurry. Do it and get out of here. If we were taking a trip driving, we didn't stop until we got there. If we stopped for gas, that made him mad. Shoot, he wouldn't sit still ten minutes.

He'd sit in a meeting, things got dull . . . zip! "They ain't doing nothing. Hell! Damn! I know that already." Then he was gone. Whatever was happening at the moment—don't care what might happen in the outcome—that's the way Sammy was. He might not eat for a whole day if something was going on. Or plan a party for a week, then wouldn't go that night. Once he wanted a new car, but his old man wouldn't buy him one. So he went down to Montgomery and cashed in about four hundred dollars' worth of savings bonds that they had been saving for him since he was a baby. He had to go and get that car.

Only thing that could keep him still was the Movement. He liked to drive, and he liked the Movement. They were the two things he liked to do, and that's what he was doing.

RUBY TAYLOR: Every time he sat down, it was Freedom. But he sure was restless. For a while, he used to tear around in that blue '61 Ford. I think it was the fastest car on campus. He had taken the gear off the steering wheel, put it on the floor, done something to the engine and made it fast. Sammy would come over to where I lived, at Rockefeller, and blow twice. That was a signal to come to the window. Plenty of nights the house advisor would come and catch Sammy sitting on our window sill, talking to me. Then he would jump in his car and fly off.

Later on he got this little beige Volkswagen, and he would drive it about ninety miles an hour with the muffler off. It was the loudest Volkswagen in town. We heard it coming, and we knew it was Sammy. Then he would blow twice or whistle and we would all fly to the window and pull up the window shades. Any time you wanted to go someplace and you ran into Sammy, you wouldn't have to worry—if you had enough nerve to ride with him.

RONALD WOODARD: One night we went to a meeting and I happened to jump in his car, a little VW. As we were driving down the highway, the first thing that came out was a bottle of wine. That was the only thing that settled my nerves, because the cat was a frantic driver.

The wine was as much a trademark of Sammy in those days as his car. But not just any wine—it had to be a certain type.

JIMMY ROGERS: Sammy liked to drink Catawba Pink wine. I've never seen him drunk, but he used to drink a lot of his Catawba Pink and he could still drive. He would drive down the street and roll his windows down and call out "Catawba Pink" and chant it over and over again. He introduced it to me and the whole campus.

LAURA PAYTON: That was Sammy's favorite song, Catawba Pink. Pink, pink, pink, pink! Catawba Pink. Catawba Pink. It sounded like a train. He and Gene Adams would walk through the Rec Hall singing that. Once they were walking around with their hats, asking everybody to contribute to the cause. People would ask what cause and Sammy would say, "To get up a fifth of Catawba Pink."

GWEN PATTON: Sammy used to work quite a bit in the Student Council office of the Institute. Well, he didn't work; he'd just be there all the time. He did help to get a lawyer for some students. One time he came into the office and was real sad about something. I asked him what was wrong, and I kept asking him, but he would never say anything. Half an hour passed, and I said, "Sammy, what's wrong?" He said, "The worst thing in the world has happened." I asked, "What's *happened*, Sammy?" He kept talking about how very bad it was. Then he said, "The state store ran out of Catawba Pink."

Sammy Younge was now twenty years old and at the end of his first semester of college. He had become actively and creatively involved in the Movement, while retaining some of his old "Lemon Younge" ways. Certainly he had not solved all his personal problems, including his fears, but he seemed to be approaching some kind of internal balance.

LALY WASHINGTON: He always used to say, "Live fast; die fast." Even before he got into the Movement, he would say, "I'm not going to live past twenty-one, and I know it." But when he got into the Movement, it was like something to hold on to, something he really cared about. It seemed like he was really going to go somewhere.

IX The Tightening Net

By late May, 1965, school had ended and there were more than twenty-five students working out of the TIAL office. Sammy was now doing less work in the county, concentrating his efforts primarily on segregated facilities in Tuskegee proper. The students' first confrontation of the summer raised a basic question.

GWEN PATTON: On May 28, George Wallace was to speak at the Macon Academy graduation exercises—that's a private white school. The newspapers said that the public was invited and we felt we had a right to go to that meeting. It was in the Armory. Wendy and his brother tried to get in, but couldn't. They came back to the office and we got more people. About a dozen of us went—there was a lot of tension there.

We almost got through but the whites lined up at the door and stopped us. They said we didn't have "invitations." There was a boy there who said, "I've just come from Vietnam fighting for freedom in this country and I can't even come into a National Guard Armory." Tears just ran down his face—and he was supposed to have been one of the outstanding men at the front. Somehow he recuperated himself. Then this whole thing about war, about killing the enemy, came to his mind. He drew a knife and said he was going to kill every white man in there and every white person he had seen. He didn't do anything, but we talked about the whole system—the war and what happened to people coming home from the war. How do they expect us to be nonviolent? We're supposed to kill the enemy over there and then coexist with the enemy here. It's ridiculous.

The rejection of nonviolence in violent America is not so recent a development in the current Movement as some people think. For the Tuskegee students in the summer of 1965, the necessity of being prepared to defend oneself against white violence was an acknowledged fact. SNCC's position there, as elsewhere in the South, had always been that local residents had the right to defend themselves and their homes. In mass demonstrations, however, the tactic of nonviolence still prevailed in Tuskegee —though its days were numbered.

Meanwhile, the students continued their desegregation efforts.

BILL HALL: On May 31, we went to integrate the swimming pool. There are two city swimming pools; one is considered Negro and the other white. Sammy was one of the people who spearheaded the drive to integrate the white pool, which we did. The white kids jumped out, and we swam all day.

JIMMY ROGERS: We had been going swimming there for two days, when one day a man approached the pool with a shoe box. He said to the policeman who was standing on the outside, "Should I?" Sammy and Wendy heard him and they asked him, should he what? The man walked away and went up onto the balcony above the pool. Then he turned the box over and a baby alligator fell into the pool.

BILL HALL: The white personnel did nothing about that alligator in the water. One of the students from Tuskegee got it out.

The following day, the whites decided to sprinkle glass on the diving board. They were fine particles so that you couldn't see them; as the students would dive off the board, they would cut their feet. So they stopped going to the board. Then the whites threw acid and manure in the swimming pool, and this was the straw that broke the camel's back. They had to drain the pool, and they wouldn't refill it.

After a while, Sammy and other TIAL students raised the question about the city pool: "Okay, it's cleared out now. Why don't you open it up again?" The Mayor and several people on the City Council responded that the town's water level was low and they couldn't afford to refill it. More time passed, and we raised the question again. One excuse led to another. A few of the Negro councilmen were trying to arrange for Negro students to use the pool on certain days and white students on others. Sammy and the rest could not accept that and continued to press for reopening. They realized that Allen Parker, who is not only the chairman of the City Council but also the president of the Alabama Exchange Bank, could be made a focus of attack. They began to pressure Parker, to picket his bank.

James Allen Parker apparently held the keys to the city.

WENDY PARIS: Parker really screwed the whole county. He controlled all the Negroes. I guess that's why we didn't get anywhere picketing the bank.

Meanwhile, the whites were bringing strong counter-pressure to bear on Sammy Younge and his family.

MRS. YOUNGE: Right after they swam in that pool, the telephone rang and the white Superintendent of the school where I was teaching said, "Mrs. Younge, I'd like to have a conference with you." First time in my life anybody in the Superintendent's office wanted to talk to me about anything. So I went in and he said, "What I have to say won't take long. I'm going to tell you what you got to do and then you get up and go out of here and do it." That made me angry and I made up my mind right then that he would hear me out too. There hadn't been any communication before, now there was going to be some.

Then he told me that he had been informed that my son was the leader of the civil-rights group. He told me all he had tried to do to get the integrated school going, and said that this group was undoing everything he had done —with all the inroads the Negroes were making, the whites would refuse to send their children. I told him, "I'm not your problem—your own race is your problem. Why is it that the burden of integration always has to be on the shoulders of the Negro? You need to go out and do some work among your own race."

"Well, I have to have cooperation," he said. Then he went on about Sammy, and I asked, "Just what does this have to do with my being an effective teacher? You think that just because my son dared to swim in a pool that I paid to put water in—and I have been paying for years— that this makes me a less effective teacher?"

"Oh, I'm not saying that."

"Well, just what are you saying?" I was trying to get him, but he was too smart.

"I'm just saying that we need cooperation."

"Cooperation from whom?" I asked him. "I think Negroes have cooperated long enough, don't you?"

Then he got angry. He called the people who went to swim "a big bunch of nasty, dirty men." He said half of the white teachers at Tuskegee Institute weren't anything but perverts. Then he intimated that Sammy was mentally ill. Finally, he said that if I didn't take some action to cooperate, I would be ostracized and criticized. I said, "Mr. Wilson, being criticized doesn't bother me. Those that want to believe lies will believe them. As far as being ostracized is concerned, don't you realize I'm a Negro?"

As in the case of the A&P picketing, it was not only whites who gave the students trouble.

LALY WASHINGTON: My mother told me, very specifically, don't go with Sammy to integrate the swimming pool. But I went. After a day or so, she found out. When Sammy came by to pick me up, she said, "You cannot go." This was the first time I was ever defiant with my mother. I said, "I'm going anyway." But Sammy told me, "If Big Laly says you can't go, you can't go." Then he talked to Mama about ten minutes. She went through this bit about how dangerous it was and I don't know why Laly wants to get involved in the Movement and I don't know whether it's just for the glory of it or the publicity or what. Sammy finally realized that she wasn't going to change her mind and he said, "O.K., Big Laly, if you say so." Then he left.

GEORGE WARE: While we were trying to integrate the white pool, there was a Negro lady going around in her middle-class community trying to get people to sign a petition so that kids from her part of town would swim in the Negro pool on Tuesdays, Thursdays, and Saturdays, and kids from the other part of town, where the poorer Negroes live, would swim on Mondays, Wednesdays, and Fridays. I finally caught up with this lady and asked her, "What the hell are you doing?" She very calmly explained to me how the kids from the other side of town drink and curse and don't take baths and they were just a bad thing for her children to be around. So she wanted to make sure that they swam in the pool at different times. There we were, trying to integrate the white pool and this lady wants to segregate the all-black pool. She had a lot of names on that petition, too.

The students did succeed in desegregating another pool at that time: the one in Chewacla State Park, in Lee County. Sammy was the first to jump in, with some fifty whites watching and waiting to see what the black people would do. But success in these efforts was much less common than failure, largely because the influential Negroes of Tuskegee did not support the students.

Sammy Younge and his fellow militants had another conflict with Tuskegee Institute's administrators in this period. A conference of black Southern college students had been scheduled for June 6–11, with SNCC as the organizing agency. The broad purpose of the conference was to bring students together so that they could discuss the problems of education in black institutions and their problems generally as black Americans. Specifically, the Southern Regional Student Conference would serve as an orientation for those committed to recruit more workers. Dean P. B. Phillips of Tuskegee Institute had given SNCC verbal permission for the conference to be held on campus.

At this time, Dean Phillips was still friendly to SNCC. Impressed by the organization's work in the 1964 Mississippi Summer Project, he had encouraged SNCC's presence on the campus in early 1965. He had in mind particularly a 1965 summer project called TISEP (Tuskegee Institute Summer Education Program), for which the Institute would receive a federal grant under the anti-poverty program. About 700–800 students—most of them from Tuskegee, the rest from the North—would tutor primary-school children in half a dozen nearby counties. Phillips felt that SNCC's experience, particularly with the Freedom School program in Mississippi, could prove useful.

During the spring, there had been several occasions on which the relationship between SNCC and the school administration was strained. One of these occurred when the TIAL students announced their intention to picket Billy Graham because of racist implications in his teachings (they later canceled this plan). The charge that "outside agitators"—meaning SNCC—were "messing up" TIAL was frequently heard. Dean Phillips must have begun to have some second thoughts about the desirability of SNCC's presence on campus.

Now a new conflict arose. TISEP was scheduled to hold its orientation on campus at the same time that the SNCC-sponsored Southern Regional Student Conference was to take place. Rumors began to circulate that Phillips would renege on his verbal commitment to SNCC, out of fear that the conference might make trouble for the federally financed TISEP program.

BILL HALL: Phillips sent a two-and-a-half-page telegram to SNCC in Atlanta, after trying unsuccessfully to reach me, saying that he had made no commitment and that he could not approve the Conference taking place on campus. Sorry. This was less than ten days before the Conference was to come off, and announcements had gone out all over the South. Phillips was in Washington, D.C.; finally, he came back and we went to see him—Sammy, Simuel Schutz, Willie Peacock, and myself. We told him that people had already been notified and we had no alternative but to go ahead. We did not tell him that we had made contacts to find other facilities. Anyway, they hadn't worked out— the churches turned us down and the Boy Scout Camp said it was "unsuitable."

Our backs were against the wall. We had to make a show of strength and demand that Dean Phillips honor his verbal commitment. We had a second meeting, a do-or-die meeting. We told Phillips that we would give him so many hours to decide, and if he didn't say yes, we would picket the administration building. Schutz said, "We're going to picket you, Dean, and you'd better believe it." Phillips said, "I believe it." He was obviously scared. Phillips was a likable puppet—it's hard to do in a nice bastard like that.

The hours passed, and we had a small demonstration. Some of the TISEP kids were arriving and Phillips called a meeting of them to say that they couldn't have anything to do with us. Since most of them were the missionary type, Establishment-oriented, they went along.

Phillips contacted us again and said we could use the Boy Scout Camp. But girls couldn't stay there overnight. There mustn't be any damage and no publicity about the camp being used. I asked him if we could come on campus for food and sleeping. "No," he said, and then, "Look, Bill, what are you trying to do to me?"

"Well, Dean, obviously we are going to have some people who are very important to us and they have to have decent quarters."

"How many will these be?" he asked.

"About fifteen." And I gave him the list, starting with King, A. Philip Randolph—the clean power boys. He believed they were really coming and arranged for them to be housed in the guest quarters. It would have been bad for the Tuskegee image to have Dr. King staying in the Boy Scout Camp. But we still had no facilities for cooking, or for girls' sleeping.

At the last minute, Sammy Younge took charge of housing and found places for people to stay. William Porter of SNCC, who was the Conference coordinator, arrived and solved the cooking problem. At the Conference itself, SNCC programs for 1965 were discussed. Among these was the Lobby in Washington, D.C. to support the Mississippi Freedom Democratic Party. The MFDP had launched a challenge against the seating of five racist congressmen from Mississippi who had been elected in November, 1964. During the last two weeks of June, people were to come from across the country and pressure their congressmen in Washington to support the challenge. This plan appealed to Sammy, probably for a number of reasons.

BILL HALL: I ran into Sammy on Highway 80; he was driving to Washington. He said, "I'm going to give 'em hell up there"—something about checking on some anti-poverty program for Macon County. He said that he would be back to work in Tuskegee. But there was still a question about whether Sammy was going to stay and work in Tuskegee or not. I think he really went to D.C. for the Lobby and to see a girl he liked, Doris Wilson. I think checking on the anti-poverty program was just an excuse. Anyway, he did stay for the Lobby.

JEAN WILEY: I saw Sammy in Washington in June. I asked him why he was there instead of in the county. He said that fighting the white power structure was one thing, but fighting the black power structure was something else, and that it drained his energy. He had to get away.

WILLIAM PORTER: By June 16, we had something like two hundred students in Washington, along with our SNCC workers. Sammy played a great part in that Lobby. He was in charge of transportation and he worked on housing—contacting people to get them to open up their homes for the students. And he lobbied himself.

Meanwhile, in Mississippi itself, a special session of the State Legislature had been called for June 14. Anticipating passage of the Voting Rights Act, the state had decided to liberalize its voting laws just enough to forestall federal intervention under the Act. The MFDP launched a series of demonstrations in Jackson to protest this maneuver and also to protest the meeting of the all-white legislature itself. Day after day, they demonstrated. And day after day, people were arrested.

WILLIAM PORTER: By June 18, about eight hundred people had been arrested. They were herded into a real concentration camp type place where pregnant women got beaten and there was a lot of brutality. One day during the Lobby, we were talking about what was happening in Jackson. Sammy wanted to tear up D.C. We had a big conflict because some people felt that the MFDP should have demonstrations all over D.C. about Jackson. Sammy was shook up because there were none. Some people decided they would go back to Mississippi, and Sammy was going down, too, to participate.

Doris Wilson, to whom Sammy had drawn closer during the Washington Lobby, was in Jackson with him.

DORIS WILSON: There were so many people in jail who had never been arrested before, who had no idea why they had come to Jackson initially, who didn't know they were going to get arrested. Then, we found people who were supposed to be in jail out walking the streets. The day we got there, we had a demonstration led by Willie Ricks of SNCC. We were supposed to have a confrontation, but things got mixed up. It was just a bad time.

The situation was chaotic in Jackson, what with the numerous groups participating, the stream of people arriving from the North who had to be taken care of, the brutality. There were also many debates over whether leaders should remain in jail or not. Sammy got involved in one of these debates.

WILLIE RICKS: John Lewis [then chairman of SNCC] was in jail, and Sammy wanted me to do something to get John out of jail. I said, "Well, that would be up to John. He probably doesn't think he should come out now." He was very upset because he liked John. To me, he had a childish way of showing his love for people. Not immature, just the way a little kid or a young person likes somebody and makes it very clear. He made it very clear that he liked John and was worrying about him. So he wanted John to get out of jail. I kept telling him how John needed to stay in jail. He sort of got pissed off with me.

Sammy was back in Tuskegee by the end of June, this time to stay. The jailings and brutality in Jackson may have frightened him into going home. Whatever the reason for his return, Sammy now seemed committed to taking on Tuskegee and its Establishment—both black and white.

As before, he attacked several projects simultaneously in an effort to find an issue which might rally the middle-class community—or a way of undercutting that class's domination. One of his first undertakings was a freedom rally, to be held in front of City Hall.

BILL HALL: He had come back from the Washington Lobby with that idea. We hoped to organize some type of group that didn't represent the authorities or the middle class and the like. The rally was scheduled for Saturday, July 17. They were going to have it with or without the permission of the Mayor, but they were seeking his permission first. His permission was granted. There were about three to five hundred people at the rally and they presented a petition with fifteen grievances.

RUBY TAYLOR: Sammy spoke about the garbage collection, and how the people who picked up the garbage were always Negroes while the white man drove the trucks. He also talked about some service station that was going to be built way out on the highway. Negroes within the city limits did not have water, but the city would spend thousands of dollars to carry water all the way out to this white man's service station. And the swimming pool—the city didn't have the water for it but there they were, going to send water out on the highway.

The question of the swimming pool, which had been raised in the early summer and had gone unresolved, finally led to a direct confrontation between Sammy Younge and the Establishment.

BILL HALL: TIAL eventually forced the City Council to have a special meeting so that Sammy, Wendy, and Schutz could ask Mayor Keever why he hadn't reopened the swimming pool. They pressured him to come out with a flat statement. Keever refused; he would only admit that he could not open that pool.

LALY WASHINGTON: Parker from the bank was there and Dr. Gomillion and a couple of other people from the TCA. Sammy had a real rebellious tone in his voice. When he addressed the Mayor, he said, "Say, man" and so on. The Mayor resented it, and he and Sammy got into this argument. Then Wendy, who was more conservative than Sammy, got upset. He and Sammy had this little argument, and finally the meeting ended with not much accomplished. Everybody had been defensive and all this antagonism had built up.

Sammy was mad with Gomillion because he was questioning Gomillion directly and Gomillion would not answer. He would nod his head or say, "I don't care to comment." Dr. Gomillion very rarely talks, anyway. But this really pissed Sammy off. He kept on. "Gomillion, you're supposed to be the leader of the Negro people. What are you doing?" Gomillion just sat there and wouldn't answer.

Sammy told me later that he realized he had been wrong. He said, "When you're dealing with this kind of people, you have to talk their language so that you can get through. You can fool them into doing what you want. I shouldn't have done what I did. But I just cannot Tom to those people."

It may have been true that Sammy Younge would not "Tom," but it would be wrong to think that he and other TIAL militants did not follow certain rules of procedure in Tuskegee. When they planned to picket someone, they talked to the person first. When they planned to have a public demonstration, they notified the police. As Bill Hall mentioned, when they planned to hold a rally at City Hall, they asked the Mayor's permission. They played the game in 1965 to a degree that militant black youths are no longer willing to accept.

But Sammy could not compromise certain basic principles. It was these principles which led to the final confrontation of the summer between TIAL's militants and the black Establishment. That story began in late June.

GEORGE WARE: We started doing something which took the people of Tuskegee by surprise. We started to try to integrate the churches. Everybody in town knew that we weren't going to integrate the churches, and that we didn't care about that. But we had moved to the point of trying to polarize the community, the white people and the black people. We figured that if there was one point on which white people in that town would not relent, it would be the church. And the black people in the community were saying, "Those white people are O.K. We can go into their churches anytime we want to. It's just that we don't want to."

So we decided to go to three churches: the Presbyterian, Baptist, and Methodist. Now, the Presbyterian Church had put out a statement saying that there could be no dis-

crimination in Presbyterian churches.* The wife of Dr.
Jimmy Henderson, who is an outstanding black scientist in
Tuskegee, decided to go down and test the white Presbyterian church on the same Sunday that we had decided to
hit all three of those churches. That was on June 27. We
didn't know about her, and she didn't know about us.

We got there at the same time, and she said, "I don't
think we have to worry about it. I have the statement here
from the Presbyterian Synod of Alabama—they'll have to
honor that." When we got up to the door, an usher was
standing there blocking the entrance. Mrs. Henderson,
knowing for sure that she was going to be admitted to the
church, pulled out her paper and read to him about the
decision that there could be no discrimination in any Presbyterian church. They slammed the door in her face.

It just freaked her out. She went home crying and said
that she would never go back there as long as she lived. She
became a very friendly force, without helping us directly.
We began to pull in people who didn't want to have anything to do with us and didn't want anybody to know that
they had even talked to us. They would call us over and
give us money at night.

BILL HALL: At the Methodist church, they were met at the
door and told, "This is not your church and you cannot
enter." One of the students asked, "What do you mean, this
is not our church? Isn't this the church of God?" And the

* In 1964, the General Assembly of the Presbyterian Church in the
United States (the highest governing court of the denomination) adopted
a proposed amendment to its *Directory of Worship*, declaring that no one
could be excluded on the grounds of race, color, or class. A majority of
presbyteries endorsed this constitutional amendment, so it was enacted by
the 105th General Assembly in April, 1965. The Presbyterian Synod of
Alabama subsequently issued a statement calling for integration of all
Presbyterian churches in Alabama.

reply was, "This is our church. Go to your own church."
The door was shut.

At the Baptist church, the same thing happened. Some
people were very disappointed because they had thought
that this would be a way for them to enter the white community and show people there can be a way of meeting one
another and talking.

GEORGE WARE: We put out a call for everybody to go to
church the next Sunday to show that we were not going
to be intimidated. We decided to try just one church—the
First Methodist—rather than all three. We also asked people
to take guns down there to protect us. President Foster
really hit the panic button then. He called in Patton and
me and said, "You can't do that. You could get people hurt.
I think it would be more noble if about five to ten people
would go down there with picket signs and just demonstrate." I said, "That's a point I'll consider," and I went
back out.

About a hundred people in the community said they
would be down there. They would be armed and they
would make sure we didn't come to any harm. Foster then
pulled in Gwen Patton and told her that I was manipulating
her, that I was going to make a fool out of her as president
of the student government. She came down to the office
very pissed off at me and said that she was going to call the
whole thing off. I told her, "Go back and tell President
Foster that I think his proposal is very good and we will
take fifteen people down to the church with picket signs if
he will agree to be one of those persons."

I knew that Foster couldn't possibly accept that, but
Gwen didn't. She went back, told him, and he almost fell
right over on his desk. He said, "Well, what do you mean?
I can't. I can't be used." That proposal paralyzed Foster, in

the sense that now he could not speak out against what we were doing. That was the beginning of our learning how to deal with some of those tricks that President Foster put us in.

BILL HALL: About five hundred people marched downtown that Sunday. They went early, to try to get there before the whites arrived. Some got in, but they were first asked to leave and then they were just picked up and thrown out of the church and back down the steps. Several whites hanging around in front of the church began to attack the people who had cameras. The ex-mayor of Tuskegee attacked a newspaperman who had a camera. One young lady, a student here, was attacked and smacked in the face, and her camera was taken away from her. But there was no attempt to attack the demonstrators themselves.

The following week, they decided to try the Methodist church a third time and to go even earlier. The church members had been changing the hours. About thirty students were going to try and get in that day, July 18. Sammy Younge, Wendell Paris, and Simuel Schutz were the principal leaders.

The police had been driving up and down the street and were stationed strategically at the corners, observing the students. Then the police left. There was no traffic. Everything seemed to quiet down. The whites, mainly men, began to gather. We noticed that they had brought bats and placed them at the corner, in the gutter, along with coke bottles. Sammy, Wendy, and Schutz walked across the street to where the whites had gathered. They stood roughly ten feet from them and observed what they were doing and then they turned away and walked back across the street to the church.

The ex-mayor's brother, Ocie Rutherford, then drove up in his car and stopped. That must have been the signal. He left on his engine, opened the car door, ran across the street, and began to beat Simuel Schutz. The mob of whites who had gathered on the corner spilled into the street and headed toward the students. It looked like two or three of them had pistols. Wendell was popped in the head with a coke bottle and had to have six stitches. I had a camera and was photographing; one of the Clyatt brothers chased me with a knife and beat me. Several of the white students were beaten. All of this action took place within a matter of five minutes. After they finished beating the students, they jumped into their cars and drove off. And within a matter of seconds, the police reappeared.

GWEN PATTON: One of the students was Donald Belton, here on the Summer Exchange Program. He was a Methodist, a deeply religious fellow who really wanted to try and reach the white community on the church level. He had had polio and wore braces—visible braces—on his legs. They beat him constantly on the spine as he was attempting to run. They just hit him and hit him until he fell to the ground. That's when they left him alone. He had to be hospitalized.

Sammy himself was attacked that day by someone he had challenged a few months before in a desegregation effort.

WENDY PARIS: A man pulled a .32 and chased Sammy and George Ware. He hit Sammy in the side with it, where Sammy's kidney had been removed. That was Ossie Ross.

He owns Pat's Café out in Lakeview. They say he's the local leader of the Klan, I don't know.

Wendy didn't say so, but it was he who protected Sammy from a fatal blow—and was badly injured in doing so. The students decided the attack had been too brutal to let the white community simply get away with it.

GWEN PATTON: We began to distribute leaflets about what had happened, called some lawyers, and swore out warrants against the people who had attacked us. We also decided to have a mass meeting on Wednesday and to bring together TIAL with the student body because TIAL was not too well liked on campus. The SNCC Freedom Singers were contacted and Malcolm Boyd, a minister from New York, was asked to come down.

It was a good meeting; everybody stayed from eight to eleven-thirty. We had people who were appealing to the community folk. We had high-school people there. We had rural people there. We had white people there. We agreed to have another try at the church the next Sunday, with a mass march downtown.

BILL HALL: One of the people who participated in the attack was the Colonial Bread delivery man. Also, two persons who worked in the liquor store. At the meeting, the TIAL students decided to demand their dismissal or else they would launch a boycott against that bread and the liquor store. Sammy would be the spokesman for the TIAL group.

Sammy asked that people begin to organize. He said, "Take your black men and organize them. Organize your-

selves and stop buying from the people downtown." He
begged people to boycott.

The battle lines were being drawn. By becoming so
involved in the problems of Tuskegee itself, and by acting
so independently, TIAL threatened the Institute's position
in the community. The Institute felt it had to reaffirm its
control over the students. Gwen Patton, then president of
the Student Body, was caught between the militants and
the school administration. She had called the mass meeting,
and the very next day she found herself summoned to the
office of the President of Tuskegee Institute, Luther Foster.

GWEN PATTON: They told me to go out and tell students
not to follow TIAL. They told me they were not really
concerned about the bloody Sunday. I was to discourage
people from going downtown the next Sunday to march
and have another try at the church.

A key issue in this conflict was the federally funded
TISEP program and its six hundred students, who formed
the majority of the students on campus at the time. Their
minds had become a battleground in the struggle between
the administration and TIAL.

BILL HALL: Dean Phillips, director of the TISEP program, tried to develop divisiveness among the students. For
instance, at one point a rumor was started that the TISEP
students had to sign an oath which said that they could not
participate in any civil-rights demonstrations or attend any
mass rallies as long as they were involved in that program.
This was a deliberate rumor that had begun in the dean's

office. There was no oath. Students were simply signing a statement that they were in the TISEP program. But it created uncertainty. Students didn't know what to do. To participate—would this mean a loss of job? Not to participate—would they be lying to themselves? It created division between the TIAL students and TISEP. When people like Sammy, Wendy, and Schutz asked TISEP students to participate or give them a hand, they would say, "I can't."

The administration also used the old argument: "You mustn't let outsiders influence you." By "outsiders," of course, they meant SNCC. The days of good relations between the Institute and SNCC were over.

GWEN PATTON: The directors of TISEP were very set on this thing called education. They wanted education to have its own concept, as opposed to the civil-rights movement. I felt that education was another tactic to keep the Negro from doing things. I had been trying to mobilize TISEP students to demonstrate, and I felt that they were ready to move.

Shortly after the meeting with Gwen Patton, the administration dropped its subtle ways of manipulating the TISEP students and made a formal declaration of war.

GWEN PATTON: Dean Phillips, who was in charge of TISEP, issued a statement that no TISEP student was to go on this demonstration or to the church. The penalty for participation was expulsion from the program. He also said that any student who went would be deported from the campus.

Some of the faculty protested the administration's actions.

MAGGIE MAGEE: Various faculty members were very concerned about Gwen going on the carpet and about what we considered the academic or just plain freedom of the students being violated. Dr. Puryear [Paul Puryear, a Tuskegee professor and local political leader] and some others went to see President Foster, because we thought that was where the top pressure 'was coming from. We tried to get him to make some statement to clarify the Institute's position on the demonstration. I don't remember much of what President Foster said; I don't think he said too much. One of the Institute's rationalizations was that since the TISEP students were participating in a federal program, they were not allowed to engage in political action.

GWEN PATTON: After hearing about that meeting, a white TISEP student from New York named Sharlene Kranz called a lawyer, and he called President Foster at two o'clock in the morning. He said that they were going to sue Tuskegee Institute if he put her or any student off the TISEP program for demonstrating. The lawyers said the students had a constitutional right to participate. So Foster called a special session of the executive council, which ruled that any student had a right to go on that march. Dean Phillips then said he was resigning.

For a few hours, the situation looked relatively good. The march took place, and in a relaxed atmosphere.

MAGGIE MAGEE: We had the march, and we also went to

the church. There were seven TISEP students there—seven out of six hundred. Donald Belton, the crippled student, was there too. The church didn't let us in so we decided to have our own service on the outside.

LAURA PAYTON: Sammy had on a suit and shirt and tie, which was out of the ordinary, and a fresh haircut. He started dividing the people who wanted to stay for the service, even if it meant going to jail, and the people who wanted to go back to campus. Ruby and I were among the people that wanted to stay and go to jail, can you imagine?

"Ruby" was Ruby Taylor, the girl who had not gone to the Montgomery march but decided that she would definitely go on the next demonstration. Nothing happened to the students that day. State and local agencies were on hand to make sure Tuskegee's image wouldn't be spoiled again; also, word was out that the Deacons for Defense and Justice, an armed self-defense group, were there. And not only the Deacons.

BILL HALL: The church crisis was the first and only time we got real community support, at least that day. The streets were blocked with cars, and there was so much lead in them that they could hardly move! These were both middle-class and poorer black people, although the real upper class didn't come. They just went to their own churches, "peaceably." But we had real protection and support that day. It was a much different atmosphere from the previous Sunday.

Back at Tuskegee Institute, however, TIAL faced a new crisis with the administration.

GWEN PATTON: Some of the students felt that Dean Phillips had been wrong when he stopped our demonstrating, but others wanted him to return. That same Sunday, about 4:00 P.M., Sharlene Kranz called to tell us that a delegation of black TISEP students had come to her room and said they wanted her out of the program. They threatened her life. Then we had a call saying that the white kids from St. Olaf's were having a meeting. They felt that we were all wrong. Their attitude was that the Negro should stay in his place. St. Olaf's seems to be a conservative, strictly Republican school. So we talked with the white conservative Republicans and we talked with the black kids, whom we could call the conservative Democrats. They marched to Dean Phillips' house, about sixty of them. Dean Phillips agreed to reconsider his resignation.

TIAL lost the battle and the Establishment, backed by students too brain-washed or fearful to challenge its authority, emerged victorious. No longer could there be any question about where the administration stood; it was clearly not on TIAL's side. "People like Sammy Younge knew that they were out there with very little administration support," Bill Hall said. Once again, they had been shown that they lacked the support of the influential blacks. The TCA had nothing to say about the church beatings except that the integration attempt wasn't sponsored by the TCA. Even Sammy's mother, a forbearing person, was outraged by the reaction of the community in this period.

MRS. YOUNGE: Except for a few phone calls and a few letters, not one local organization made a statement about the church attack. With all of our organizations—fraterni-

ties, sororities, all the groups which had civic programs—
they didn't make one public statement about the church
thing. Not one. This is a case where I don't believe an
individual would have been as forceful as a group of
people. A group lets the community know where you
stand. Some statement should have been made about re-
sorting to violence.

GWEN PATTON: Sammy, on many occasions, tried to appeal
to the local Negro leadership. We had gone to their meetings. They couldn't understand Sammy and the others at
all. They began calling them all communists. Sammy was
ostracized.

WENDY PARIS: During the summer, Sammy wrote a letter
to the TCA saying something like, "You got to let us in
somehow—we'd like to have a meeting with you, and see
if we can come up with some kind of constructive plan of
action." We never did get an answer, or if we did, I never
did see it.

"TIAL has done a great deal to set back the progress
which the town had begun on its own," stated *The Southern Courier*, a newspaper sympathetic to so-called civil
rights. "If Tuskegee is so great, why can't we go to church
together?" asked Sammy Younge in *The Activist*, a student publication started that summer. But Sammy's voice
did not prevail. The white violence was the fault of the
black students who "insisted on all or nothing": so argued
white "moderates" and the Negro Establishment. Sammy
and others in TIAL were even isolated from people who
had once been close to them on a personal level.

LALY WASHINGTON: By this time, Sammy and I were so involved in the Movement that we got completely alienated from most of our old friends. People we had grown up with called us wild and crazy.

Given the Negro Establishment's opposition to the students, it came as no surprise when a grand jury failed to indict those whites arrested for the July 18 attack at the church. Despite the black majority in Macon County, the grand jury on the case contained only two black people out of eighteen members. This, too, failed to arouse the Establishment. In such a climate, racists felt they had been given a free hand.

BILL HALL: Some time after the beatings, three girls from TIAL went to the Dairy Queen, a white drive-in. They were met by some white fellows who said derogatory things to the girls, brushed against them and the like. The girls went back to the TIAL office to report this. A few minutes before they got there, Sammy's mother called. Someone had just telephoned her and said, "We're going to bomb your home." We rushed over to the Younges'. Sammy tried to get police protection but couldn't.

WENDY PARIS: He called me and said, "Look here, man, they coming to my house." I got up and went down there. He and Stevie both were out there with guns, waiting for the people to come. I got in his car and went to sleep. We stayed about an hour, maybe, and finally realized there wasn't nothing coming. Man, I think it scared his mother half to death. We stayed out there about two or three days, watching the house day and night. Other people did, too.

BILL HALL: Unlike a lot of the Tuskegee youth, Sammy drank and partied with the grass-roots people. They liked him—so he called people to stand guard and they came. The Deacons for Defense came, too. They guarded the house day and night for about two weeks. People who drove through that block had to be identified before passing Sammy's house.

MRS. YOUNGE: I was angry with the kids as much as anything else because even after being beaten, they were still going down to the Dairy Queen and what not. It could have been a very serious situation. This is when I called the Mayor and told him that not just for the sake of our children, but for *their* children, he needed to put some police protection at places where their children meet and could possibly get into some difficulty. A situation of this kind should never have existed in Tuskegee.

Sammy was very upset about the bomb threat, which was the first of several. His father, then working in Atlanta, came to Tuskegee only on weekends so that his mother was alone with her younger son, Steven, during the entire week. Sammy therefore moved out of the SNCC "Freedom House" where he had been living and back into his home. He even talked about leaving Tuskegee and going to school in the North, so as not to endanger his family. At the same time, he seemed unable to give up challenging racism and exploitation.

LALY WASHINGTON: Sammy and I used to slip off and go to Montgomery without our parents knowing anything about it, just testing places. Once we ran off to Auburn and tried to go in the Holiday Inn to eat lunch. The man said,

"This room is reserved for a private banquet." Sammy got mad and said, "Private banquet, hell. I saw you lock the door when we came up. What are you trying to do?" The guy called the cops, but nothing happened. They just told us to leave.

This kind of drive to confront whites can be the result of frustration: organizers who get up-tight in waging a complex struggle against a massive power structure will sometimes go off on their own to have an individual, simplistic confrontation with the enemy. But Bill Hall, who worked closely with Sammy Younge, saw his drive as part of the youth's tendency to spread his energy too thin.

BILL HALL: Sammy and I were having a problem ourselves in this period. He was too active. He would work one area and then do something else. He was too busy being active to be an organizer. I wanted to see TIAL operate as an organization whereas Sammy would just do certain things, try and develop them, try to get others involved. I wanted very much to try and help develop a person I knew had fantastic potential. He had so much energy. He was overflowing with energy. And imaginative. We lived together for a month in the Freedom House. We had altercations. You can call it immaturity or my inability to express what was inside of me. Anyway, I never could translate to Sammy what I felt his capabilities were.

Another example of Sammy's impulsiveness, his attempts to do too much, had come up when TIAL first established its office in Tuskegee.

ELDRIDGE BURNS: We had money in TIAL, maybe a thousand dollars at one time. Sammy had big plans—the telephone was really a big thing with him. But then we had only a hundred dollars left in the treasury and that's what the telephone cost. Sammy was mad at me 'cause I wouldn't give him the money. I said, "Wait. Let's get some more money first." He stayed on me and stayed. So I finally signed my name, but he had to have two signatures. He went downtown and he changed the account so he could sign instead of the other guy. He got his telephone. And the 'phone bill came and there were a lot of long-distance calls on there. "Man, you know what?" he said. "We shouldn't have got that telephone right then 'cause we didn't have no money to pay for it."

Certainly, Sammy Younge had his weaknesses. But his dominating characteristic was an inability to tolerate injustice, a constant compulsion to fight racism. It was that quality which made the whites of Tuskegee declare him their enemy in the summer of 1965.

BILL HALL: Sammy had become a target. He could be identified just through that beige VW. We were very conconcerned about that, and after a while we simply insisted on Sammy putting his muffler back on. Wendy Paris also had to get rid of his truck, because of an incident that had occurred when they were working on the school question.
    Tuskegee has two high schools—Tuskegee Institute High is the Negro school and Tuskegee High is the white school. We got information that the city fathers and the Uncle Toms were going to try and petition Negro students into the white high school that fall, to desegregate it. Sammy was disturbed about the idea that they had hand-

picked the kids. Also, he believed in people going to the school that's closest to you. The kids who had been hand-picked were from the "good" side of town and really closer to the Institute High School.

He got hold of an application form for transfer, and we made about a hundred copies. He had people going from door to door, particularly in the poor community, to get people interested in applying. We simply were not going to sit back and let thirteen hand-picked students enter that all-white school. As a result of all this, we did manage to get about fifteen others in.

One evening, we were driving home some of the young kids working with us on this. Wendy had his Ford panel truck—the only Ford panel truck in the community at that time, I think. We called it the Freedom Truck. We were coming back through the white community, and as we passed a car we heard a loud noise of crashing glass. We stopped and went back to see what had occurred. The front windshield of a parked car had been busted by some type of pellet. That pellet had obviously been meant for us. The police stopped us, arrested Wendy and two other fellows for no reason, and took them to jail. Wendy's old man bailed us out. We realized then that the truck was a target. They knew about TIAL. They knew about Sammy.

The net around Sammy Younge was becoming visible. The pressures were becoming almost intolerable. Yet even that summer, he continued to show his capacity to relax and enjoy life.

GWEN PATTON: There were a whole lot of things that Sammy thought about, and most people didn't realize it. Many times he would just sit down and contemplate. But then he could really get wrapped up at a party. Let himself go, forget about certain things. He liked to dance, and he could sing real well—he had had a singing group with a little band behind it, before he became very active in civil rights.

LAURA PAYTON: We had a dance that summer in the gym. Sammy was dancing with Betty Gamble and I was dancing with Wendell. We were doing the "Boomerang." The noise that Wendell and Sammy could make when they were together—it was out of sight. When the record was over, Sammy stood in front of the floor and hollered, *"Uhuru!"* Other Movement people, who knew what it was, joined in. I asked Wendy what it meant, and he told me, "Freedom Now" in Swahili. We had a real blast that night.

Then came the final incident of the summer, the experience that would make Sammy Younge try to stop the wheel of his fate.

BILL HALL: One of Sammy's frustrations that summer had been that he couldn't get the voter-registration drive in the county off the ground. The demonstrations in Tuskegee kept a lot of students in town. Another problem was that students got no money for working on voter registration with TIAL, but they did get paid for working the government-financed TISEP. So the voter-registration drive sort of died out. But during the latter part of August, Tom Millican—a white student at Auburn University in Lee County—asked TIAL students to give them a hand with voter registration in Auburn. Of course, Sammy agreed.

They held several mass meetings in the White Street Baptist Church and decided that on September 1, the legal registration day, they would transport people from Auburn to Opelika and then on to the Lee County seat. A church in Opelika would serve as a refuge where the people could stay overnight before going on. There were, I think, sixty-four people going to the courthouse. All of them were arrested in Opelika, along with seven TIAL students—including Sammy.

We felt the arrests should be enough to arouse the Opelika community. But the black community folded. We couldn't get any of the ministers to visit the people in jail. Most of our lawyers were in Jackson, Mississippi. We heard that Tom Millican had been beaten; we couldn't get the Negro doctor to him. People didn't know what was happening inside the jail and we couldn't plan anything effectively on the outside. Finally, Wendy's old man came into Opelika and bailed out the TIAL students. This was Sammy's first time in jail. It frightened him; it really frightened him.

Sammy and the rest of the kids felt that they had to follow up, go back to Auburn. He was forced to make a decision. Could he continue to go back to Auburn and lead the people, knowing how he felt about being in jail? Or should he just cut himself off? That's what he began to do. He wouldn't go to Auburn. Wendy and Schutz and the others were traveling, but Sammy wouldn't go. He wasn't a coward, but he had one kidney and a blow to his side could be fatal. That was constantly on his mind. Any type of physical contact had to be avoided.

In addition to his physical problem, Sammy must have been thinking about what had happened to Jonathan Daniels only a week or so before. Daniels was a white theology student from the North who had been working with SNCC in Lowndes County, Alabama. He had been arrested during a demonstration there. On August 20, 1965, a deputy sheriff shot Daniels to death just as he was coming out of jail. In 1964, three civil-rights workers in Mississippi had been murdered after they had left jail. That might be the way the net would close in on Sammy, too. One way or another, he knew it was there and could tighten at any time.

ANN PRATT: I used to talk to Sammy about his drinking and he would tell me, "Don't worry about my kidneys. I won't die because of them. I'm going to die from a bullet. Somebody's going to have to kill me."

X   The Last Decision

JEAN WILEY: When I got back to the campus in September, Sammy had on a suit. A gray tweed suit, I think, very stylish, with a vest, a tie, shined shoes, and a hat. I was shocked because the Sammy I knew was very casual. I asked him, "What is this new image?" And he said that he had decided to be a little more serious about school. When he said that, though, he didn't give me the impression that he was at all satisfied.

I also began to notice that he was drinking heavily— just wine, but he was usually sort of high and I had never noticed heavy drinking the whole time he had been working with the Movement. I asked him about it a few times and he just said, "Well, you gotta have some kind of outlet." Then he would walk on. I noticed that he wasn't mingling with the people he'd known before. He seemed to be trying to detach himself.

GWEN PATTON: He came into the office and told me, "Gwen, I'm going to school. That's the purpose of me being here at Tuskegee Institute." I couldn't believe it. It was a parody of what people always said. Then he went into my office and got a piece of paper. He pecked it out on the typewriter—his resignation from TIAL.

He said that he wanted to form an organization called SPAT (Student Political Action Team). It would be a correlated thing to TIAL, of education and politics. It was basically great, but I believe that Sammy was really trying to get out of TIAL. He disassociated himself from Simuel, Wendy, and everybody. He'd come in our office every day, helping students, but that's all.

ELDRIDGE BURNS: He said, "Man, let's don't work in civil
rights this year. I'm tired, man. We're going to study this
year." I said, "Okay, man, 'cause I'd like to get out of this
place some time this year."

Everyone agreed that Sammy was trying to detach
himself from the Movement, but as to why, there were
various opinions.

GWEN PATTON: He was permitted back at Tuskegee Institute on probation because he hadn't carried enough hours
during the first semester and his average was lower than
that of people usually allowed to return to school. They
didn't say he couldn't involve himself in civil rights or he
would be kicked out of school; they just said, "Remember
you're on probation. Therefore it's important for you not
to involve yourself in civil rights."

ELDRIDGE BURNS: I think his trouble was that there wasn't
anybody really active in civil rights around there just then.
Nobody cared.

LALY WASHINGTON: The way I figure, it was really based
on Karen. She wanted him to finish school, get his degree.
They were still going together off and on.

STOKELY CARMICHAEL: He invited me out to a party in
Tuskegee to drink some wine. It was a lawn party, with
those higher-ranking Negro people, and he was all dressed
up. We started drinking and he told me, "Look, man. I'm
gonna kick SNCC. I'm quitting. I want out." So I said,

"Well, all you got to do is just be out. There's nothing to it. You just came and you're just out. No membership, no dues, no cards, no nothing." So he said, "I can't take all the pressures, you know." He began to drink more wine, and as we talked some more, the shit started to come out. The pressures from his friends—fraternity-type friends—it was too much, being with SNCC.

DORIS WILSON: Sammy was feeling really frustrated and he was worried a lot about his mother, about how they were maybe going to blow the house up. His father wasn't too happy about his relationship with the Movement, especially SNCC. His mother was not the type who would force him to do something he didn't want to do. She just wanted him to do something constructive.

School, friends, family—all these may have been factors in Sammy's decision. But there was something else, which both included those factors and went deeper.

GEORGE WARE: Sammy, Wendy—a lot of those kids who wound up in TIAL—were kind of like renegades from their society. There was something different about them all the way. Before they got involved in the Movement, they were the so-called hell-raisers in that town. They were just a lot more independent than the rest of the kids. But something happened to Sammy at the end of the summer. The Tuskegee system got to him.

"The system got to him"—that is probably the best way to explain the change in Sammy Younge in September, 1965. Sammy was the sum total of his environment;

he contained both its paralyzing restrictions and its unusual potentiality for freedom. Doris Mitchell, one of Sammy's teachers, said he was the freest middle-class child she had ever seen in Tuskegee, and she probably spoke the truth. But Sammy also grew up breathing the air of a status-conscious society which preferred big cars to big ideas, a society whose watchword was "don't rock the boat," a society in which respectability was everything because it seemed to be a means of survival to some black people. He could not be entirely free of that society's pressures—especially when resisting them meant not only ostracism but also danger to his life. Sammy Younge was trapped by the community, inside and outside himself.

BILL HALL: The middle-class community never gave Sammy a real opportunity to be the free person he was. He had found people he could relate to, in SNCC and in the Movement generally. But a Movement doesn't operate in a vacuum. It is based on a community. The community just wasn't ready and this Sammy discovered over the summer months. The community made it impossible for Sammy to organize. Things were moving in all directions, but nothing was coming together. Without an ideology, without a sense of how movements work, you go back to the most familiar and least uncomfortable thing. In his frustration, Sammy could find no alternative except to go back to school. His drinking points to his whole situation. Probably, it made more sense for him to live in a bottle than in that community.

I left Tuskegee just before school began, because there was nothing I could say to him at that point. We needed some time to pass, so that we could look back.

Sammy's decision represented an individualistic solution to a problem that was deeply political. Not surprisingly, he just flailed around in school.

ELDRIDGE BURNS: For the first couple of weeks, we used to go to the library and study for about five minutes and then get up and go someplace else. Just a big fake. One day I said, "Well, man, I think I'll go back out in the country. I think I'll go up to Brownsville." So we rode up there and he talked to all the people he had organized up there. He came back and said, "Aw, man, I ain't going to mess with that stuff." So we left it alone. He'd jump in his car and go to Atlanta, Montgomery, Columbus, or Birmingham, or any place.

Then one day he withdrew from school. He said, "Yeah, man, don't tell my mama, but I withdrew from school." I said, "What did you do that for?" He said, "Oh, man, I'm tired. I haven't been studying. I can't make it."

The next day he said, "Well, man, I'm not going to withdraw from school. Shit, I think I can make it all right. I just want to get an *A* in math. I been progressing in math. The first test I made a 32; the second test I made 33; and the next test I made 36." He started laughing. All I know is that he hadn't opened his math book for maybe two months. He'd say, "Well, man, let's go out to the house and study." By the time we'd get there and start studying, he'd start drinking wine and that would be the end of that.

We were playing basketball at the high school one night. We had a community team, a bunch of winos that didn't go to school. He had to turn in a paper in sociology the next day, so he ran up to the library and got a book— something about Africa. He wrote on the paper the word, "Africa." That was about nine o'clock. So then we had a quart of wine.

Sammy's withdrawal from the Movement brought him little satisfaction; it did not even end the threats to his life.

LAURA PAYTON: One day we were walking to the dorm and this white man in a car stopped us, or stopped Sammy. Sammy told me to wait, and when he came back, he said, "I guess I'm going to have to start carrying my gun. You know, that guy could have gotten both of us." I said, "What did he want?" "Oh, he stops me all the time," Sammy said. "He wanted to know where the Homecoming parade is going to pass. He just wanted to bother me."

On the last day of September, there was a sudden— but temporary—break in Sammy's new pattern of life. The murderer of Jonathan Daniels, Deputy Sheriff Tom Coleman of Lowndes County, had just been acquitted.

GWEN PATTON: Sammy came into the office that day and he said, "Gwen, what are you gonna do about Jonathan Daniels?" I said, "Sammy, I thought you had quit civil rights." He looked at me and didn't say anything. He walked out of that office and got a coffin from somewhere. Then he wrote a sign saying "Alabama Justice" and he put it on the coffin and said, "This is to symbolize justice in Alabama. We're going to demonstrate."

Sammy planned a march with the students for Jonathan Daniels. We called a meeting that night and Sammy was the spokesman. Afterward, we went back to the office and we stayed up all night long. Sammy helped draw up a letter to the students and organized the march. He drove around town and gave his reports and all that. We had maybe sixty students marching downtown to the Confederate statue. Sammy was the main marshal.

WENDY PARIS: He started going to Brownsville again, taking people there. But very seldom would he go out there by himself at night. He knew they were at him. He knew they were at him!

We went down to Pat's Café one night, again trying to get in there. Rutherford walked up. He's the man that always pulled a gun on me. "You got your pistol there, Mr. Rutherford?" Sammy asked. And about that time, he had it out. So we got on back across the street 'cause we didn't want to start nothing. We came back a little later on, and Rutherford came back again. "I'm gonna shoot you," he said. And he actually told Sammy that he would get him that night. In fact, he followed us down the road.

Sammy soon pulled away from the Movement again, although he kept in touch. When Jimmy Rogers of SNCC came to Macon County to try and organize a "Black Panther Party" like the one in Lowndes County, Sammy sought him out and gave him a lot of ideas. But he told Rogers that he had too many personal problems at that time to take on any responsibility himself. Through the months of November and December, Sammy stuck to this position and turned his attention to clothes and parties. He also moved a couple of times during this period.

ELDRIDGE BURNS: He went to Charleston in November. He saw his cousin with a blue pin-striped suit like Al Capone used to wear. So he said that he had to have a suit like that. We must have gone everyplace before he finally found it. So he had a blue pin-striped suit, and a white tab-collar shirt, and a blue-and-white pin-striped tie. He used to put on that little hat and throw it to one side and stand up like the gangsters, rocking back and forth. Another day, we went all over the world looking for these wide ties. We were going to start a fad. His father had a whole box of them, so we put them on and went to a football game. People called them shirt protectors. We had everyone wearing those wide ties.

About that time, he got tired of living at home. Everybody was trying to watch him. So he got this little house, and we went to live there. We got us a stove, and we cleaned up that stove, and we cleaned up the house. We were fixing to have a big party on his twenty-first birthday, November 17. We invited all the parents to come out—my parents, Sammy's parents. They wanted to see what kind of an apartment Sammy was in. So all these old people came out there and brought glasses and skillets and a big cake. It just seemed like they were going to stay forever. It was a Wednesday night, and all the girls had to be in by 10:15. The old people stayed and stayed and stayed. Sammy said, "What we gonna do, man? What we gonna do? What we gonna do?" They finally left, and we went on and had our little party.

STOKELY CARMICHAEL: He was high that night, and we had a talk. He said he was putting down civil rights. He wanted to get into the bag, and he was going to be out for himself; that was what he was going to do. So I told him, "It's still cool, you know. Makes me no never mind." He said he thought a lot of SNCC people were putting him down because he was going back into the bag, but that didn't make any difference to him because cats put him down when he went SNCC. I told him that I thought there would be some people who would do that, but as far as I was concerned, we could still drink wine any time.

Apparently Sammy got tired of living out at the house with Eldridge Burns and one day suddenly decided that he was "going to be a good boy, going to be where his mother and daddy wanted him to be," as he said to Eldridge. He moved back home. Christmas rolled around; Sammy had a quarrel with Eldridge about money, but they made up and spent the holiday together. The next day, Sammy went to Birmingham alone to see a girlfriend. When he came back, about two days later, he happened to talk with Scott B. Smith, a SNCC field secretary.

ELDRIDGE BURNS: Scott B. really got to him. We were getting ready to go out to the county the next day and Scott B. made some remark to Sammy: "Remember, when you don't come around, the girls come around." I think he was half-kidding Sammy—that other people would work Brownsville if he didn't and that those powerful female organizers would take over. But Sammy really felt bad about that 'cause the people in Brownsville were something he cared deeply about. The next day, everybody went out into the country together but Sammy went by himself up to Brownsville. He was pretty excited about it.

JIMMY ROGERS: The next thing I knew, Simuel Schutz and Wendell Paris called and told me Sammy had been out in the Brownsville area again talking to people; that he planned to have a mass meeting soon. They said even though it had been some time since he had been out there, the people still worked with Sammy.

Over the holidays, we talked about it and went up to "Little Texas" where he had been working some during the last semester. Out of all the people we had, he was the best known up there. We decided that he would work in "Little Texas" and that we would work in other areas.

Sammy Younge was in motion again. He had left the "model town" behind him once and for all. Stokely Carmichael, who remembered his previous turning point, recalled this one too. It was a period of intense repression in nearby Lowndes County, with black people being evicted from their homes for registering to vote and other political activity.

STOKELY CARMICHAEL: On December 30, we were putting up tents to house the people who had been evicted. Sammy came over to help. He just drove up one day. He had on his dungarees, overalls, jacket, everything. I said to him, "What's happening, baby?" He said, "I can't kick it, man. I got to work with it. It's in me." We talked a little, but there was so much to do that we didn't talk too long. He just said that he had tried to kick it, but he couldn't.

He decided that from then on, he was going to push harder and do everything he could. He realized that the cats in college weren't shit and they weren't going nowhere nohow. So he had to work with people that were ready to work, and the people ready to work were in SNCC.

Sammy was interested in the idea, which he had discussed with Jimmy Rogers, of building an independent political organization in Macon County like the Lowndes County Freedom Organization. He discussed this with Stokely before leaving Lowndes on New Year's Eve.

STOKELY CARMICHAEL: I said, "Well, all you got to do is talk about building a Black Panther Party in Macon County. See how the idea will hit the people and break that whole TCA thing." He said he was all for it. What he wanted to do first was just go and get a lot of Negroes registered outside of Tuskegee proper. He was going to start pulling in those people and hold meetings and see if that would lead to a Black Panther Party. My own feeling was that it would. I just told him that he had to be careful about how certain people projected themselves at those meetings. That was it. He left.

The night he got killed, January 3, they called me and told me. It was about 1:30 A.M. and they said I should come right away. I didn't have any strength, man, so I just got me three bottles of wine and drank one for me and one for Sammy and one for Jonathan Daniels.

XI   Death of a Myth

The last day of Sammy's life—Monday, January 3, 1966—had begun busily. It was one of the two days a month on which people could register to vote in Macon County. This gave Sammy an opportunity to plunge into a favorite activity.

ELDRIDGE BURNS: Monday morning, Sammy had come back from Birmingham, just like old Sammy again. He walked around town saying, "What we going to do is this..." You know, planning again. "You go on this corner; I'll go on that corner." Get all these people to come down here by the Jitney-Jungle, to go register.

I said, "Sammy, I got to go take a test right now." It was eleven o'clock. He said, "All right, man. I'll tell you what to do. Yo go on and come back at one o'clock and everything will be okay." I came back at one, and he was on the street corner. "Come on. Let's go, doctor. Let's go."

JIMMY ROGERS: We had brought a lot of people down to register—we had 118 people at the courthouse. The registrar decided that he wasn't going to register people because we had too many down there. He said he had to "purge" the list that day—take off the names of people who had died or moved out of the county. I asked him, "Couldn't you find some other time to purge the list? Today is registration day, and we only have two registration days a month."

"We're purging the list, and we have signs saying so posted all over the courthouse."

"I'd like to see those signs." He pointed at the door of his office. "I don't see any sign," I said.

"We're not going to be registering people today." He just kept on saying that.

I said, "Well, you're going to be registering us today."

"No I'm not, because we're purging the list today."

"If you don't register us today, I'm going to find out why." He walked back to his office. The people started to leave, and I told them not to because he was going to register us. When he came back he said, "Well, okay. Seeing that you're here, I'll register you. We'll purge the list another time." About five people went in to be registered, and I jumped in line. I was the sixth person. I filled out a lot of unnecessary papers and then when he read the oath, I questioned it.

"We don't understand that. Could you break that down because I noticed a lot of people seemed to be puzzled." I asked him certain questions—I don't remember what.

He said, "You've been causing me trouble all morning. If you don't get out of here, I'm going to spill your guts all over the floor."

"What did you say?"

"I said if you don't get out of here, I'm going to spill your guts all over the floor."

I said, "O.K. I'll see about that." I went to the telephone and called the Atlanta SNCC office and had them call the FBI and the Justice Department. While I was gone, Sammy had come up with Eldridge Burns and Wendy Paris.

ELDRIDGE BURNS: I guess maybe sixty or seventy people were standing there. The place was crowded. One guy kept making people move, telling them to get out of the way. I went up to get the names of the people who were registering. Wendy and I said to the registrar, "Listen here,

Doc. You got to register more people than one man every twenty minutes, you know. These people have been up here since eight o'clock, and you didn't start until ten-thirty." Then the registrar pulled out his little knife, which was red and yellow.

WENDY PARIS: "I'll take this knife," he said, "and cut your guts out. Spill your guts on this floor." Old Sammy came up and asked the man's name. The man said he gonna cut his guts out and call the sheriff on us.

ELDRIDGE BURNS: Nobody was afraid of him. He was too old to do anything, at least in the daylight. So I said, "Man, put your knife up."

JIMMY ROGERS: When I found out about it, I told Sammy that he should call the SNCC office, too, and tell them about the knife. So we rode to a café, and we contacted the office again.

WILLIAM PORTER: I was on the switchboard at that time in Atlanta and got both calls. We asked Sammy for some additional information on the incident. He couldn't give it to us at that time; he said he would get it in later.

JIMMY ROGERS: When we got back to the courthouse, there was an FBI man already there. He called me off into another room and questioned me as to what had taken place. I told him. He then asked me had any of the local officials been notified. I told him that I didn't talk to any of them. Later I found out that Sammy and Wendy had talked to the sheriff and some of the city policemen, who said they couldn't do anything because it was outside their jurisdiction.

The FBI man decided that he would meet with us the next morning. We went to the Freedom House in Tuskegee to have a staff meeting. Sammy came in later, but he stayed only a little while. I told him that I would like to talk to him before he left, but we were so involved with the conversation that he left and I didn't notice that he had gone.

Sammy had gone back to the courthouse to continue helping people with registration. At about 5:15 P.M., they had finished.

ELDRIDGE BURNS: We left the courthouse and I went to pick up Sammy's mother with the car. Later on, Sammy met me again. We went down to the store, got some wine. I left him at about a quarter to seven that night and came on home.

AUFAIT WIIIAMS: About seven o'clock, Sammy and this fellow Gene Adams came by the dorm. We were going to have a party out at Gene's house. Sammy said they would be back at about eight to pick us up.

I had been to a lot of parties but that one was the best. They had some bongo drums and Sammy got up and danced. That was the first time I saw him dance. He was picking us up and playing and carrying on—he seemed happier than I had ever seen him. About ten o'clock we got hungry and decided to cook. They had some chicken but they didn't have any meal. We put some rolls in the oven and fried some bacon while Sammy went out to Mertz to get some pork chops and bread. The first time he went out, he took his girl with him. They stayed at Mertz a while and then came back. We had started making some tuna fish and didn't have any mayonnaise. Somebody needed cigarettes. So they decided to send Sammy back out again to get cigarettes and mayonnaise. This time he went out by himself. Before he left, he was standing at the door talking and jiving with everybody.

WENDY PARIS: We were having a meeting at the Freedom House. Sammy came by about eleven. He had been at some party. We were teasing around and I put a red Black Panther sticker on his car. They had just come out, it was something new.

NORMAN "DUKE" BARNETT: I was at the meeting, too. I didn't have any shoes on and Sammy was teasing me, "Hey, man, what you got your foot out for?" I said, "Haven't got any money." He told me, "I got thirty dollars coming, I'll give you that and you get yourself some shoes and some clothes." Then he left.

AUFAIT WILLIAMS: The second time he went out, he didn't come back. And we didn't know what had happened to him.

Eldridge Burns and others who had not gone to the party told about the confusing, frightening sequence of events that followed.

ELDRIDGE BURNS: About twelve or twelve-thirty that night, somebody called. I was asleep and my mother answered the phone. They wanted to speak to me, but she said I was asleep. A few minutes later, somebody called again. My mother thought it was one of the guys telling me to come to a party, and she wouldn't wake me up. Then my father picked up the phone, and somebody—he didn't know who—yelled, "Sammy's been shot." That's all the person said. Right after that, Sammy's mother called and said to come over there. She thinks Sammy's dead. She thinks somebody shot him.

We went over to the house. Stevie was yelling, "They killed my brother. The white man got him. I told you they were going to get him, didn't I? I told you they were going to get him." But we didn't know for sure whether Sammy was dead or even where he was. My father got on the phone and called the filling station downtown, the bus station, the police station, the Veterans' Hospital, the white hospital downtown, all the private doctors. And nobody knew. We couldn't get in contact with Wendy. Stevie had a two-way radio and started calling around to see what he could find out. Then I went to look for Sammy.

JIMMY ROGERS: One of the people that Stevie called on his two-way radio was this fellow at the Texaco station. The fellow came to get us at the Freedom House—Wendy Paris and his brother, Simuel Schutz, Ron Woodard, and me. He said that Sammy Younge had been shot, and we asked him, "Where is Sammy?" He said that he had heard that he was somewhere near the Greyhound bus station. We jumped in the car and went down to the bus station. When we got there, we saw Stevie and Mrs. Younge and four or five policemen standing by Ed Wilson's Standard Oil station, which is right next to the bus station. Sammy's car was parked near the door of the bus station where you buy your tickets. We got out of our car and asked the policeman, "Where is Sammy?" He said that he didn't know.

WENDY PARIS: I opened Sammy's car and looked inside but didn't see anything. I looked for shotgun bullet holes, and I still didn't see nothing. I asked the Chief of Police, "Where is Sam?" He didn't say nothing. I said, "We heard he's been shot. Y'all better hope, you better hope he's not shot, 'cause if he is, all hell is going to break loose in Tuskegee and you know it." I was about to go into hysteria 'cause we knew something was wrong.

JIMMY ROGERS: Then a taxicab drove up. Schutz ran to the driver and asked him had he seen Sammy or heard about anybody being shot. The cab driver was looking out of the window talking to Schutz and he said, "No, but what's that body doing over there?" Schutz turned around and saw that it was Sammy, lying in a dark spot in the driveway between the gas station and the bus depot. He yelled up the street, "Wendy, Wendy. Come here, Wendy. Come here."

WENDY PARIS: I think Schutz and my brother held me, and they went over there, too. We saw him, lying in that pool of blood. I saw his eyes, open, and I knew he was dead. So I ran back and grabbed his mother, put her in the car, and told my brother to take her home.

JIMMY ROGERS: The fellow from the Texaco station went and got a camera and came and took some pictures. About an hour and a half later, Dean Phillips and Dr. Puryear from Tuskegee and Stanley Smith from the V.A. and a lot of policemen and other people, some of whom we were able to recognize as public officials, came down. We told them that something had better be done about this or there was going to be trouble. We stayed there for a long time. About two or three hours later, it seemed, his body was moved and we left.

ELDRIDGE BURNS: At the Younges' house, Stevie kept shouting. "I knew they were going to get him. I told you they'd kill him, didn't I?" His mother was in a state of shock. She kept saying, "They got him. Them crackers got my boy. They got him. I guess it'll be Stevie next and then it'll be me." And she walked around all night, just back and forth. Sammy's father came in, and he was all upset. He said, "Stevie, I had me a good cry before I left Atlanta. So you go and get yours out." But Stevie and his mother still never shed a tear.

Later on, people started coming in, and they came all times of the night. His father told me to pick the pallbearers that Sammy might like. I thought we all should be honorary pallbearers because I knew I couldn't carry the casket. Wendy couldn't either. It just would have been too much.

That was that, you know. I really didn't have any feelings at all about it until the funeral because I didn't believe that it was true. I hadn't thought about it very much because I knew that Sammy would come blowing around. "Let's go see about buying a car." Or, "What's going on, little man? Let's go get one. I got the dollar, you got twenty cents?"

Sammy Younge had been killed by a single bullet in the back of the head, at approximately 11:45 P.M. on January 3, 1966. There was no question about who had killed him; the man admitted it soon afterward. The basic story of what had happened that night emerged from the reports of several witnesses.

GWEN PATTON: I've read five affidavits, and they all say basically the same thing about what happened. It seems that Sammy was at the gas station that evening when a group of Tuskegee students drove up into a sort of alley between the gas station and the bus depot. As far as they could gather, he was going in to buy a package of cigarettes and he also asked to use the restroom. The man at the station, a white man, pointed to the back. The bathroom for Negroes is there, the one for whites is inside. Sammy said—they heard him say this—"You haven't heard of the Civil Rights Act." Sammy wasn't going around to the back. Harsh words were exchanged and the man started waving his gun. He told Sammy to get off his property.

Sammy got in his car and moved it over near the bus station which is next to the gas station. There's a cab-stand there, too. They still had this exchange of words. At that point, the man waved the gun and then raised it. There were some golf clubs standing beside the bus station—they belonged to a passenger waiting for the late bus to Atlanta—and Sammy pulled one out. The man looked as though he was coming at Sammy. Sammy ran and the man fired. He missed.

Sammy ran onto the Greyhound bus standing there—the bus to Atlanta. He shouted, "Would you shoot me on this bus?" The bus driver got off and went to talk to the man, told him he'd better not do that. Sammy got off the bus and it pulled away. But those students were still there. Sammy was still running, trying to get back to his car. The man raised his gun again and shot. Sammy fell, hit in the head. There are some very strange things about all this. I can't see Sammy walking off the bus voluntarily without having had some type of satisfaction. Sammy would have torn that whole bus up rather than walk out there and face a bullet. I believe there must have been some type of exchange, that nobody's talked about, between the bus driver and the gas station man, which made Sammy think there wouldn't be any trouble. Sammy wasn't afraid to go out and do something that needed to be done, but violence upset him a great deal and the consequences from violence really disturbed him. I can't see Sammy, twelve o'clock at night, aggravating or agitating somebody, like they say.

Others who knew Sammy well agreed on this point.

WENDY PARIS: People say that Sammy was standing there, cussing the man out. Saying, "You won't shoot me," and all that. But that wasn't the Sammy I knew. And he wasn't drunk. I know he wasn't drunk because I had seen him about forty minutes earlier and had put that sticker on his car. That's probably what did it.

ELDRIDGE BURNS: Call him nigger, send him to the back, he wasn't going. He was going to sit up there and tell you he wasn't a nigger. You treat him like a man. That night, Sammy was talking right back to the man. The thing must have just built up in him. He must have known that this was his night. He just told the guy, "You don't treat me this way." He probably cursed him.

But I know that when the stuff got rough, Sammy wasn't going to sit up there and argue. I just know. When he went to jail in Opelika that summer, he was nervous the whole time. I know Sammy was not sitting up there wolfing with that man when that man had a gun in his face. Sammy was gone. And the man had to shoot him in the back.

The question of what Sammy said that night at the station is, ultimately, irrelevant. He had been shot and killed in cold blood by a sixty-nine-year-old white man named Marvin Segrest because Sammy Younge was a black who refused to stay "in his place." Segrest even admitted firing at Sammy and was arrested shortly after the killing, then released on bail. Naturally, white Tuskegee would try to say that Segrest had a "right" to shoot Sammy. This old, familiar tactic was designed to justify outright murder of blacks by white racists and has sometimes even confused fellow blacks.

But it was not just the whites who had doomed Sammy Younge to death—and who now acted to protect his killer.

GWEN PATTON: Who is really the cause of Sammy's death? Whose hands are really bloody? The white people downtown knew that the TCA, which is the Negro leadership, didn't like Sammy. That gave them extra leeway to intimidate Sammy, Wendy, and Schutz. If the TCA had applied any pressure to the city fathers, nothing would have happened to Sammy. That's why, when the TCA went over to Mrs. Younge's house to express their sympathy, she said, "When my son needed your help and asked for your help, you weren't here. Now, he's dead."

ELDRIDGE BURNS: There's a Negro attendant down at that gas station. After the murder, they kept him constantly drunk and nobody understood why. He was always mumbling, "I saw it. I saw it." But then when some white people looked at him, he would say, "I didn't see it. I didn't see it." He saw, but if he tells, the white man's gonna kill him. He knows that, and he doesn't want to die.

GWEN PATTON: I want to know why those Negro students in the car couldn't have pulled Sammy in with them and taken him away. They drove off, man, and left him. They circled the block and came back—by then, of course, everything was quiet.

*

Sammy Younge was not the only casualty of January 3, 1966. A myth also died that night: the myth of the "model town." Beneath the surface of Tuskegee's calm "biracialism" lay white violence and black fear—racism in all its forms. Now the mask had been stripped off. Sammy Younge's work while alive, and the way he died were a message to Tuskegee: face reality and move on from there. As long as you live a lie, nothing will truly change. We will remain slaves, even if we call ourselves free.

The mask was off, but people still had to acknowledge the reality that had been revealed.

XII   "What We Gonna Do?"

In the first days following Sammy Younge's death, many people, shocked and angered, moved to action.

WENDY PARIS: The first thing was violence—I was about to tear up Tuskegee right then. First time 'bout to lose faith in the nonviolence movement. So we made some Molotov cocktails, we were ready to throw 'em. Somebody told us to sit down and think a little while. We thought and decided the best thing we could do is to show Tuskegee, show Tuskegee to the world. I don't know how nonviolence got tied back up in it, but the next day, we had a march.

GWEN PATTON: They called me at three o'clock in the morning to tell me that Sammy was dead, and I laid the phone down and went upstairs to my room in the dormitory. I stayed up, 'cause I realized that even though Sammy was my friend, there was something I was supposed to do, and I had to figure out what it was I could do. So I sat there and sat there, and about five-thirty I decided that I would have a meeting in the gym at eight o'clock in the morning. And we decided to march that same day—Tuesday. About three thousand people turned out.

RUBY TAYLOR: Everybody went on that march—students, faculty, community people, all marching in the rain on downtown Tuskegee. I wasn't there, but I heard about Gwen reading a statement to the Mayor and the City Council at City Hall. She talked about the swimming pool and the churches and the stores, and wanted to know what they were going to do. But Mayor Keever [C.M. Keever] just "deplored the incident" and promised to help bring justice. Then the Mayor and the councilmen sang "We Shall Overcome" with the marchers. Yeah.

While the Mayor was busy deploring, the crowd was shouting, "That's good, but what are you going to do?" and "We've heard that before." To back up the demands for reforms, members of the Tuskegee Institute faculty and student body formed an organization called the Ad Hoc Committee for Justice in Macon County. That committee's first public proposal opened by saying that Sammy's murder was not "merely the isolated act of one depraved individual" but "symptomatic of much deeper and pervasive evils in the community. We are far from the 'model' community that some would insist that we are."

The next day, Wednesday, Sammy's funeral took place and there were no demonstrations. Marching and picketing resumed on Thursday. A meeting was called that day by Luther Foster, the Institute's president. In a packed hall, Foster proclaimed the freedom of staff and students to involve themselves as they desired in civil-rights activity and stated that he expected "that people will so involve themselves." It seemed as though the Institute administration finally shared the students' militant spirit.

Then the pressures of Tuskegee began to be felt again. So-called community leaders were saying, "Let the police take care of things," "Don't demonstrate," "You know Sammy probably had an argument with that man," "Sammy might have been drunk"—the same old attempts to rationalize inaction, to justify irresponsibility (the real kind, not the type for which militants are always being criticized). The number of marchers dwindled rapidly.

WENDY PARIS: Some people in the community felt that we should have marched the first day and after that it was

all over. Just another man dead, people said. Some felt we
had taken it too far—we were messing up this little so-called
ideal city.

One morning, a man working with the TCA came to
the house to talk to me. "Don't march today . . . let us talk
before you march. If you got to march, let us talk about
two hours." I didn't talk with him, I left him with Dad,
went on and led the march. That man was Palmer Sutton,
Sr., whose wife had once been one of the key witnesses
in the suit to desegregate the schools. Somebody must have
got to them. When we start marching or doing anything
all these people don't like, they say it's a SNCC takeover.
That's the best excuse they have around here—a SNCC
takeover.

GEORGE WARE: One time, during the marches, Willie
Ricks got up to speak and started saying it was the City
Council that killed Sammy Younge. And Gwen tried to
stop him. I said, "Now let Willie Ricks speak!" Every time
Ricks would start, people would say, "No, no, Ricks."
"He is going to cause too much trouble."

On Friday evening, the newborn unity of administration and students met an early death.

GEORGE WARE: Gwen Patton called a meeting of the entire
student body for Friday night because the administration
said it had been informed that on the next march the highway patrol would come in and use violence—things like tear
gas or something. We had been going down every day and
the whole thing was becoming more and more tense. At the
meeting, Dean Phillips said that people could get hurt if
they went downtown. My point of view was that if there

was real danger, the president should move to eliminate that danger. He had a lot of power in the community and he could do something about it. But instead he counseled people not to go.

Now, we wanted to start a whole pressure campaign, to get the franchise taken away from the cat who owned the Standard Oil station where Sammy was killed. We wanted to call on everybody at this meeting to turn in their Standard Oil credit cards and get other people to do it. Then this joker started saying "I don't think you should cause a lot of people to suffer just because some guy got killed." This cat was talking about the fact that there were a couple of Negro Standard Oil stations in Tuskegee. Some people shouted him down and then there was a big hassle over whether he should have the right to speak or not. Dean Phillips was saying we should be courteous and democratic and all that.

I could see that the students were beginning to be turned off by the meeting—the lack of coordination and everything. But I just couldn't marshal my thoughts, I was too angry. Wendy was very good—emotional, but controlled. He blew that cat away. Then Jim [Forman] got up and kind of flipped things back over again by talking about Sammy, and saying that the issue was whether we would go downtown the next day or not. He asked the students, "What do you live for? That's the basic question, baby." President Foster kept talking about how he couldn't tell students what to do, he was for students making up their own minds, but there was very real danger if students went.

Dean Phillips had also been doing a very funny thing behind the scene. He was trying to isolate me, taking the position that I was not a student because I had come down from my job in New York. But I told him I was as involved as anybody else. I wasn't going to get caught in that bag.

That Saturday, the students went ahead and marched.

GEORGE WARE: Because of the way that meeting ran, we didn't start out with a lot of people—maybe 250, although there had been about 1,500 people at the meeting. We walked them down the street, and the city police had a barricade across the road. It was very funny, 'cause it was obvious that these cops didn't have any experience in stopping a lot of people from doing anything. They had never had billy clubs before. But they were standing there in their white helmets, looking militant. When we got to them, Sheriff Sadler said, "You do not have a parade permit. This march will not proceed." That was the first anybody had said anything about a permit.

So we moved over into the middle of the street and sat down. This news was transmitted back up to the campus and students began to pour down there where we were all sitting-in.

Now, there was all this wheeling and dealing going on between President Foster and Allen Parker, the president of the Alabama Exchange Bank, who is also on the City Council and who also controls the police department. There was constant telephoning between them. Dean Phillips came down and said: "Look, things are getting very crucial. The president would like you to come up to a meeting." I said, "Well, no, I ain't gonna do that. I'll send Butch Cabiness. He's articulate, he knows exactly what we're going to do, and he can go up and talk with the president."

I knew about Foster's meetings. All week, he would call key people in and hold those damn meetings for twelve hours. This would be after a demonstration, where people had been involved in a lot of exhausting things all day long.

He would keep them in there until three or four o'clock in the morning so that they would be too exhausted to discuss what they were going to do the next day. Finally, people got hip to that and just decided that they weren't going to any more of Foster's meetings.

Butch went and talked with the president, who said, "You got to stop the students because if they go downtown there's white people with guns and people could get killed." He didn't keep Butch very long because he had wanted me up there; he thought that if he could get me and Wendy out of that group, then Phillips could handle it.

Then there were these guys from the Federal Community Relations Service. They had this integrated team working with Dean Phillips to try and put an end to our thing. People kept saying, "We want to march. We want to march. We want to march." They decided that they would line up again and march on through the police line. Then the cop got a call on his radio. Just as we were getting ready to move forward, he came back and said, "Wait a minute, I'd like to say something to you. You all can march downtown." Foster had told Allen Parker that the students couldn't be stopped and no harm had better come to the students. Foster said that only because he knew what would happen in that black community if people went down there and got hurt.

What we wanted to do was to tie up the whole business block, which was owned by Allen Parker and other influential whites. It was Saturday afternoon and we could freeze up that whole business area. Essentially, that's what happened—we just sat down in front of the stores.

Over a thousand students, joined by county blacks who had come to shop and stayed to demonstrate, halted business for an hour and a half. Then the students marched back to the campus quietly. Over the weekend, at a meeting called by Luther Foster, a fourteen-point proposal was drawn up by TIAL, the new Ad Hoc Committee for Justice, and U.S. government officials. The fourteen points included demands for federal examiners and other measures to step up voter registration; a civilian review board; hiring of additional black policemen; a positive school-desegregation plan; an ordinance prohibiting segregated public facilities; investigation of welfare policies and practices; the addition of black names to the jury rolls.

Beginning on Monday, January 10, students repeatedly picketed City Hall and the County Courthouse to press those demands; a teach-in was also held at the town square during the week. On Saturday, January 15—a week after the sit-in at the downtown stores—the demonstrations drew to a close.

LAURA PAYTON: We were heading downtown that Saturday about 1:00 P.M. I was kind of disturbed at first that the number of people was so small—only about twenty—but when we started marching and began to sing freedom songs, I figured that this was just one of those times that any number would do.

After we got downtown, we formed a picket line in front of the Alabama Exchange Bank, all the way down to Danny's Clothing Store. We covered that one block. We had our picketing signs. This was, strangely enough, my first picket. I didn't have any gloves; it was cold and raining. People started complaining, but we continued walking around in a circle. After about thirty minutes, Wendell decided that we would move across the street, in front of the City Bank, because there were about ten Negroes standing on the corner looking at us. We said, "Look, brothers and sisters, come on over and join us. This is your fight, too."

RON WOODARD: When we marched down there, we were thinking about our small number and how they could whip some heads today. They wanted a SNCC member up in front, so I'm up in front and I'm thinking all kinds of things, like these white folks are gonna start shooting on us. They were ready, too. Cars kept circling the square— one of them was driven by the same cat who beat up the students at the Methodist church the summer before. They were waving guns around. The cops did their usual nothin' about it.

WENDY PARIS: The trouble started when George Jackson, a white fellow who owns a drugstore, tried to push through the picket line. He shoved William Scott, a student. Then a cop said Scott was under arrest for assaulting Jackson.

RON WOODARD: All the rest of the cats ran over there. The cops ran too. One of them shouted, "O.K., who wants to fight?" Another one took off the latch that holds the gun down, and everybody went for it. Three cops grabbed Wendell Paris. They had Wendell Wilkerson too, and he hit back.

Some white cat came out of an office, rolling up his sleeves, asking for trouble. He said, "Look at these niggers out here," and somebody niggered him clear across the street. Cats had cops by the hair and everything. Some white fellows came up in a car. When one of them opened a shotgun, this cat broke the car window with his hand trying to grab the guy. This white guy was so nervous, he couldn't put any shells in the gun.

My nonviolence had went home that day. Some old

cop walked up to me and said, "I'm gonna tell you what to do." I said, "Fool, you ain't gonna tell me nothing today. Tomorrow you might, but today is my day here. We finally decided that this is our downtown and you white folks ain't got nothing more to do with it. We're tired of you all." More cars started coming up after that. A white lady jumped out of a car and she said, "You goddam niggers. You nappy-headed buzzards." Then she got back in her car and rolled up the window. The cops see this type of thing and they don't say nothing. But the minute they see niggers getting together, that's when they hit.

LAURA PAYTON: I panicked and dropped my picket sign and just stood in the middle of the street and started screaming. I was supposed to go over there and help them, but I was so scared, all I could do was scream. Then I got myself together and went over to where a couple of deputies were standing on this curb. I said, "You're chicken, that's why more than one of you got to fight a man, because you aren't men. You're just scared." I decided to go back and tell the kids on campus what was going on. I walked back to school, went into the Rec, and was telling somebody that they were down there beating up Wendy and it's a fight. Wendy was chairman of TIAL. A guy playing cards said, "Ah, girl, go on." I said, "What do you mean, go on? One of our students is down there being beaten up and you talk about go on. What's the matter with you, man?" When I said this, everybody got up from the table and went running out.

   We got a ride downtown. On our way there, we saw about five hundred people marching in orderly fashion. Dean Phillips was down there trying to tell some people to go back to the campus, we can't have this; then he looked up the street and saw these five hundred people coming.

Dean Phillips said to me, "You girls better go back across the street because it looks as if there's going to be trouble." Just then, this blue car came around with four white men and we could see one of them in the back seat, either loading or unloading a gun. You could even hear the sound. One of the students pointed it out to the cops, but they didn't move. So half the crowd starting throwing bricks at the car and rocking it. In about a minute, everybody had gathered around this one car. The man had it in reverse and he was driving backwards. Then people just started running and throwing bricks and beating out window panes with umbrellas.

RON WOODARD: What happened is that folks started asking the black people in the stores, "Didn't they ask you to stay out of these stores? You wouldn't listen to us. Now we're going to ask you again to get out of these white folks' stores." These were community people, mostly; I think they weren't so much mad at the cops as they were mad at seeing those people in the stores after we had done all that work telling folks not to shop there. One of them said to a man going into a store, "I ain't gonna ask you no more," and he picked up a huge brick. An old lady inside said, "I got a bad heart!" But he threw it anyway, and she came out of the store. They all came out.

LAURA PAYTON: Dean Phillips was trying to tell us to go back to campus. Wendy and Eldridge and some more TIAL people were up on the statue out there, in the square, trying to decide if we should get a rope and pull it down. So we said, "We have a boycott on the town, where we gonna get the rope or the chain to pull it down with?" That presented a problem. Then Dean Phillips got on the loudspeaker and said we should go back to the campus. Everybody was asking Wendy if we should. By now Wendy had decided it was best that we go back.

RON WOODARD: The cops lost their cool that day. They weren't thinking. Most of them can't think anyhow. There's a cat on the police force who can't read. He told one guy to write down his name and the man wrote down a name. The cop went back to the police station and showed it to the captain. The captain said, "Fool, he done wrote *your* name down here."

The next day, Sunday, we had the last march. Finals came up, and that was a good excuse. See, the biggest response we had got wasn't from the students at Tuskegee; it was from the people in the community. But after the excitement died down, the students went back to the same old routine. I think they knew they were responsible for what happened. They felt that responsibility for a while, but when they had the excuse that more people weren't supporting the action, they got away.

The weeks that followed the demonstrations were a time of turmoil—not so much on the streets of Tuskegee as in the minds of its citizens, particularly the students. The naked fact of a racial murder in this "model town" was the main reason for the students' growing alienation; but there were others. Shortly after Sammy's death, SNCC chairman John Lewis had issued a statement on the murder in which he said: "If the federal government cannot provide protection for people seeking civil rights guaranteed by the Constitution, then people will have no protection but themselves. We find it increasingly difficult to ask the people of the Black Belt to remain nonviolent. We have asked the President for federal marshals for over three years. If our plea is not answered, we have no choice." A few days later, agents of the FBI came to talk with the SNCC people in Tuskegee.

SCOTT B. SMITH: The FBI came by the Freedom House and asked, "Where is Jimmy Rogers?" Jimmy was asleep but he woke up and they began to ask him about the Lewis statement. Meanwhile, students were coming around to prepare for demonstrating. We told the FBI to call up Washington, D.C., right now and tell them that we have no other choice if we don't get federal protection. The FBI would take us outside to talk and some of the students would go along. They kept on asking, "What are you going to do?" and we just said, "You'll see." Finally, we said we wouldn't go outside again. They stayed for an hour. There they were, watching us—not the Klan.

Right down the line, the federal government behaved as it always had when a black man was killed in the Deep South. The students did not fail to note that when Reverend James Reeb had been killed in Selma, the President put his private plane at the widow's disposal—but for Sammy, a black man, the White House didn't even send a message of condolence. Furthermore, Gwen Patton's letter to the President—worded in such language as "Please, sir, understand our feelings and give us all some type of satisfaction" —brought only a cold, self-defensive reply, not from the President, but from the Department of Justice. The racism implicit in these contrasting responses fanned the flames of anti-white feeling on the Tuskegee campus. As for

Sammy's murderer, Marvin Segrest, he had been quickly apprehended but the grand jury was taking months to hand down an indictment.

The Tuskegee activists were also disturbed and alienated by the attitude prevailing among many of their own fellow students.

ANN PRATT: Some people are walking around as if this thing has made no kind of impression on them in one way or the other. I just don't see how they can do it. I mean, Sammy is somebody we all knew—if not personally, by sight anyway. I don't see how they can walk around as if nothing has happened.

EDITH GORDON: In the dormitory, I can't see how the kids just walk around. Especially those from Alabama. I'm not from Alabama, I'm from Texas—but Negroes have it bad everywhere. I have a girlfriend who has to be in at twelve because it's not safe for a Negro to be out in Birmingham after midnight. I couldn't live like that—and they're satisfied with it. You check the marches and about a fourth of the people are from Alabama. The rest of them are from outside. One girl asked us, "What are you demonstrating for?" I don't understand it. A Negro. An Alabama Negro.

AUFAIT WILLIAMS: You can't make the students see what you've seen. If you wear an Afro, kids classify you. But they don't classify you as one of the hep; they classify you as wild and foreign and all this jive. Even some of the instructors—if you come into class with an Afro and you've been doing *C* work, you have to do *A* work to get a *C*. That's black instructors—not the white instructors, they're the only ones who accept you. I don't know whether it's because of fear that you're going to harm them in some way.

RON WOODARD: I want to know what it's going to take to get these people over at Tuskegee Institute to join. People ask me, "Why did you join the Movement?" I say, "For a lot of reasons." Because you've seen an idea there and thought you could build from it. They haven't seen this idea yet. When somebody busts them up 'side the head with a brick, or they're called "nigger" enough times, they might catch it.

Too many of them talk all that old nonviolent stuff. Or else they say, "I can't get involved in it. I'm not nonviolent." Nobody has even asked them about that. "I'm not nonviolent. I'm not going to let nobody hit me." But you find out where they're from—they're from someplace where they've been called "nigger" all their lives. What it really means is, they're afraid in so many ways. Not the fear of being killed, because I don't believe they think in terms of that too much, but afraid of really facing themselves. Afraid of finding out that they're really not as much as they seem to be and want to be. It's our fault too, in SNCC, because we haven't given those students a program. When I say students, I mean a couple who look like good potential. The majority of them ain't in nothing but the way.

The student attitudes reflected those of the black middle-class community as a whole, of course. That community, with some exceptions, seemed little changed by Sammy's murder in the first month after it occurred.

ELDRIDGE BURNS: Black people in this town are still trying to take up with these white people. They say: "Well,

Sammy's dead. Let the law take care of it." Hell, if the law *had* taken care of it, then you know Sammy wouldn't have been dead.

Some people are finally realizing that Tuskegee isn't what they thought it was, that the Man's still beating them. My old man worked as personnel manager out at the V.A. for about ten years. They gave his job to a white man and wanted to transfer him to Vermont. All the Negro heads of departments at the V.A. are being transferred. So he quit. I think he's finally coming around to see and understand better. I told him I didn't want to live to be fifty-one before I saw. But I feel sort of happy about my father. Now he sees that there are things I have to do, and he's back of me.

But most of the Negroes in this town still think that everything's fine. It's going to blow over. CBS is going to come back and do another thing on this model community of Tuskegee. People here don't realize that tomorrow if their son goes down to that station, he's gonna get shot. And if I go, I'm gonna get shot. And brother, I'm not going! Really, I can't take no more of it. Fine, I really want to demonstrate and I feel that we should do it in a peaceful manner. But I'm tired of it, you know. I'm really tired of it. I'm tired of getting pushed around and then having old people sit up and tell me what I should or shouldn't do. Same thing they told Sammy.

It's bad when you get it from the people who are supposed to be the black leaders of this community. I'm sick and tired of people afraid to trust black people when they're black people themselves. If you can't trust yourself or black people, why trust the Man? The Man hasn't done nothing for you. They don't understand. They're afraid to put themselves in a position where they'll have to make decisions. I could make some decisions. I know a lot of other people who could make some. I'd rather see Wendell

Paris be mayor of the town than Keever. But, they don't see that, because Wendy doesn't wear white shirts and pretty ties. His hair isn't cut enough. He doesn't speak with the "best of language" and all this kind of stuff.

RON WOODARD: They talk about "you SNCC kids." It really bugs me to hear that. "The SNCC kids." I remember when I was in CORE and we used to be "the CORE kids." When a demonstration comes up, they say, "Well, I'm supporting you." Then I go out and get my head cracked and they say, "We're sorry." All the years they've been in the world and they haven't done anything. Or else they think we're a bunch of gods—we give up everything to be in the Movement. I really flip over that.

I was surprised to hear a lot of people out in the community, youngsters, talking about "I'm already free." It made me kind of sick to hear them say that. They say it without really thinking about it. Another thing! I was talking to some people the other day about the fact that we don't want to go slow. A lot of people in Alabama tell their kids that, in time, everything is going to be all right. And the kids repeat that. Go slow, like the whites say. Some people say they're fighting for their kids to be free. Well, I'm not. I'm fighting for *me* to be free. I want to see it in this day and age.

Sammy Younge's mother and his seventeen-year-old brother, Stevie, reacted to these community attitudes in their different ways.

MRS. YOUNGE: I say to my friends all the time, "You sit up here in Tuskegee and you think you have the world in your hands." Unfortunately, we have on our side some who will sell their souls to gain favor—and not only inter-racially. I don't say this is an attitude of our people—I imagine it happens on both sides—but it's something we've had to resort to, to get as far as we've got. You know, the TCA never did issue a statement deploring Sammy's murder.

We should help our young people and help each other. But we're too busy talking about what they're doing wrong. Nobody helps our colored children to organize, to get things financed. They have to go out in the street and hold cans. We've been labeled by others, and within our own group we have labeled each other. I don't like labels. We abhor each other. We fight each other. We haven't got to the point in life where we can see that it's only in unity we can live.

SCOTT B. SMITH: Stevie wanted to kill Segrest, there's no doubt. His mother tried very hard to calm him down. Finally he volunteered to go into the Air Force. I think he wanted to get away from the town—from what had happened, forget how the community was relating to it, the people he thought were family friends, who did not back us up. This hurt him very much. The whole attitude was "Let's forget about this, let's don't say anything about this whole problem." I think he also felt very guilty that he hadn't been more involved before. But the town's attitude after the murder was what disturbed him most.

As for the white power structure of Tuskegee, its position changed about as much as that of the black power structure. The Ad Hoc Committee for Justice struggled on—drafting new city ordinances, attending meetings of the City Council and Board of Education, urging Attorney

General Richmond Flowers to be prosecutor in the Sammy Younge case, submitting names of black citizens eligible to be placed on the jury rolls, collecting affidavits of police "unfairness and inaction" to support their proposal that a new Commission of Public Safety be appointed, urging blacks to register to vote, and so forth. But these activities bore little fruit in the first half of 1966. As Gwen Patton put it, "That was a phase—and maybe it was a phase of non-substance."

WENDY PARIS: The proposals all got filed away, except that the Justice Department closed one restaurant—The Lakeview—and Pat's Café is integrated. Gwen and I have been in there.

JENNIFER LAWSON: I quit school in February to work with SNCC in Lowndes County. I always knew that I would drop out of school because, at this point, it was useless and irrelevant to me. There I was, a biology major, sitting in a classroom learning about the green stuff that grows on trees while there are people out here who like to hang people from trees. So, this little green stuff that grows on trees had no relevance in life at all. I couldn't see the classroom situation unless I could apply it to my everyday life. And I couldn't do that.

My first year in school, I had been a typical Tuskegee student. I was in the dormitory and ate my meals in the cafeteria. I didn't have to leave campus for a thing. It's all provided for you right there. But I could see that there was so much in life I was missing. You pass a shack coming into Macon County on your way to the school, but that's sort of irrelevant to you because you're coming to the campus where you're going to be in a nice warm dormitory. If somebody's outside in the cold, it's not your problem. And then the answers people give you in terms of what you're moving toward. You're moving toward the fact that some-day you'll be able to afford a nice house and a nice big car, and I just couldn't see that being everything. So I started looking for the answers myself. Like, what am I living for? Like, what meaning does my life have?

Then, during the summer of '65, I worked a nine-to-five job in New York, for cancer research. I had all these great promises of how, when I finished school, I could move right into this top position, and how the institution would pay half my expenses if I would go to Cornell and work on my Master's. It was really a great life. But while I was up there working this nine-to-five job, I was reading everyday about Jimmy Rogers and Ruby Sales down in Lowndes County. All the while, I felt out of place, be-cause I should have been in Lowndes County. I should have been in Alabama. When Jonathan Daniels got killed I felt I should have been here.

The first semester back here at Tuskegee, I worked with Jimmy in Macon County to ease my conscience about not being here over the summer. Most of the kids in school are working toward the day when they get their degrees, and then the first thing they talk about doing is leaving the South for good. In school, you learn to exclude people—and these people are just like your parents and your grand-parents. They live in shacks and they're "nasty." People go to school and they get in these nice little middle-class posi-tions and then they can't talk to their grandparents or to their parents because they're ashamed of them. You go to New York and you forget the South is here. But I plan to live in the South.

To me, this is just a big classroom right here in Ala-bama. I'm still reading a lot; I can read things now and see what answers a particular author has for the problems.

There are some changes I can bring about myself, by being out in Lowndes County. If I do nothing but get more students involved, that will be something. In a classroom, you hear all about the great theory of democracy and you swear that it's working. Out here, you know it isn't. This is where it really is.

EDITH GORDON: We have to blame ourselves, too, for Sammy's death. Last year, when TIAL really got active on campus, everybody was saying: "I have to finish school first. This is what I'm here for." But I feel right now that a semester or a year out of school is not too much for me to give up. Not now. I'm sorry we had to wait until it happened so close to home.

Not everyone dropped out of school. Some of the activists continued their studies but with a new kind of consciousness and commitment.

WENDY PARIS: We've lost a lot of faith and confidence in people that even Sammy would have talked to. It doesn't make any difference, though. Back during the summer, we were trying to work, trying to pacify, trying to get along with the Tuskegee community. We sent out little letters— "If something's wrong," we say right nicely, "well, tell us." Now we don't care at all. We can't help these people here no ways. They don't need it that much, they got money and they got a car. So we're going to work out in the county where we should have been all the while. 'Cause they want help, and need it.

One of the students who felt most strongly about carrying on Sammy Younge's work among the rural people of Macon County was Ruby Taylor, the girl who had not gone on the Montgomery march a year earlier.

RUBY TAYLOR: After Sammy's death, although I had been working with TIAL (maybe not as much as I should have) I found myself getting more and more involved in the Movement. I felt that after Sammy had got killed, I just couldn't see myself sitting around doing nothing. I've heard of a lot of other cases where Negroes were shot down in the street and nothing was done about it. The next person might be me or my closest friend.

We began a ten-day registration drive, canvassing from door to door out in the county. In Fort Davis, Springhill, and other areas, we got about eighteen hundred people to come down to the courthouse to get registered and pay their poll tax. People who didn't have a way to get to Tuskegee we would transport back and forth. Ricks was here with his station wagon and Jimmy Rogers with the white Plymouth station wagon and other people would let us use their cars. For a while the Ad Hoc Committee for Justice in Macon County paid for the gas and food.

The murder of Sammy Younge even had a radicalizing effect on Tuskegee youths away from home. Laly Washington, Sammy's friend from childhood, had heard the news in a bus station while on her way back to Fisk University after spending the Christmas holidays in Tuskegee. At her mother's insistence, she did not return to Tuskegee but continued on to Fisk.

LALY WASHINGTON: Willie Ricks called me from Atlanta when I got back to Fisk. He asked me to organize a memorial service for Sammy on the steps of the Capitol in

Nashville. I told him I would try but that it would probably be futile.

I went around the dorm and got as many people as I could to say they would go. I went and bought all these black arm-bands and put them on as many people as I could see. All over the campus. I tried to get people to go downtown the next day. It was raining, and I got two people to go with me down to the Capitol. I called the press but no press showed up.

I couldn't get one, not one, of Sammy's friends from Tuskegee who were at Fisk to go downtown. They said things like, "I have a class." Or, "My hair will get wet and I don't want it to get messed up." I was cursing and hollering and screaming. We walked halfway into town and hitchhiked the rest of the way in the rain. I cursed all the way there. It was terrible. We stayed there for two hours on the steps of the Capitol, in the rain.

When that didn't work, I said, "I'm going to try to arrange a service at the church, the Episcopal church. Maybe more people could get down there since it's closer to Fisk." I made posters and I put them up in the Student Union and all over the campus: MEMORIAL SERVICE FOR SAMMY YOUNGE, WHO WAS SHOT IN TUSKEGEE AT A SERVICE STATION FOR TRYING TO USE THE WHITE RESTROOM. I guess about ten people came to the church. It turned out that about five of those ten people just happened to be down there to study. There's a Student Center there and they just came on in the church.

Sammy's so-called friends at Fisk made me so mad. Then I found out that some SSOC* people had tried to get down to the memorial service, but had got the time mixed

* Southern Student Organizing Committee, a group of antiracist white Southern college students.

up. They hadn't made it and they were very upset. Willie had told me on the phone to try not to get any white people, if I didn't have to—we were trying to get soul folk, which I agreed with. The thing that really pissed me off was that all these white folks from SSOC were concerned and really wanted to come, and all I could get was two blacks from Fisk to go down to that memorial service. This was one of the key things that made me decide to work with SSOC in Nashville. They were the only people that showed any kind of real interest.

Sammy's death made me feel that I had to quit school and work for the Movement. I couldn't study anyway. I went home and talked to my mother about what I'd been doing. It was amazing. Not that she was glad, but she said, "That's what I felt you had to do." That I was going to find myself, as she puts it. When I wrote her that I definitely didn't think I could go on in school, she was with me. Now she writes me every week. She sends me literature on community organizing materials.

She has little basic discrepancies, like wanting me to leave my hair long. And she was very concerned about my getting involved with SSOC, because she didn't know whether it was a communist group. That was her one objection. She told me to get off the National Committee for Alternatives to the War in Vietnam, because I might be labeled a communist and this would hinder what I would be doing and what jobs I might want. I tried to get the point across to her that I wouldn't want the kind of jobs where I would have this kind of security clearance anyway. She wouldn't listen to that and she said, "Well, your husband might want a job with the government and your being on this list, etc." She ran all this stuff down about how the niece of former President Patterson of Tuskegee

Institute had been involved in some kind of communist-type group and so he had got into all kinds of trouble. There's no need for my just worrying her, but I'm not going to back down on my convictions.

Some people talked about doing things that spring and did them; others just talked; still others continued to struggle silently with the question of what to do with their lives. It was a time of anguish and confusion, those early months of 1966. But the feeling about one of our brothers having been killed never faded away completely. There were the students already mentioned, and then people like Ernest Stephens, George Ware, Simuel Schutz, Warren Hamilton, Kathleen Neal—all of them bearing an unspoken devotion. Their feeling about Sammy's death was like a dynamo, sometimes working and sometimes at rest. But always capable of being activated.

WENDY PARIS: Every day I think about Sammy. Other people've forgotten. I can sit down and talk with him now. Boy, we carry on a general conversation—well, you know, it's just in my mind. But sometimes I'll be sitting in class and just talk and laugh with him. Or whenever I'm by myself. I want to drive all those people crazy now. That's about what Sammy would have done, I guess.

JEAN WILEY: When people first heard Sammy was dead, they were running around and crying and asking, "What are we gonna do? What can we do?" And we're still asking that: "What are we gonna do, what can we do?"

Sammy was just a beautiful person, and we cannot, I swear, we cannot let Sammy's death be in vain—not in

Tuskegee, not in Alabama, not in the South, not in this country. I don't know what we're gonna do, and I've often asked myself what Sammy would do. I think I know. He would get up and he would go about his work, as he defined it. And he would let the others just talk, as he did so many times in the past.

XIII   The Promise of Spring

As winter drew to a close in Tuskegee, nothing much seemed to have changed on the surface of political life. Yet there were faint stirrings, a new sound here and there. On February 3, 1966, a Conference on Alabama Justice took place; it was sponsored by the Ad Hoc Committee for Justice as an effort to examine the "shortcomings" (to put it mildly) of Alabama's legal system, to determine what could be done about them, and "to rededicate ourselves to the task of doing what must be done."

The conference took the form of a vigil, beginning at 8:00 P.M. and lasting until 4:00 A.M., with speeches and workshops. Attorneys and civil-rights leaders from both North and South attended. It was at a workshop of this Conference that Tuskegee had its first public discussion of independent political organizing for control of local power —the kind of movement which had been evolving in Lowndes County and which would take concrete form a few weeks later with the creation of the Lowndes County Freedom Organization. (Tuskegee had seen an effort at independent politics two years earlier, in the Non Partisan League headed by Dr. Paul Puryear, but its emphasis was not on black control.) The idea did not go over well in Tuskegee generally; among student activists, it became a cause for further dispute and division.

GWEN PATTON: Bill Howard, a student on campus, believed that a Black Panther Party could work in Tuskegee. He wrote a long editorial in the campus newspaper. The majority of TIAL members thought that a Black Panther Party couldn't work here because of the structure of the community. The bourgeois people and the poor people didn't have any unity. But Bill really thought it could work, and that caused division in TIAL.

Another source of division in this period was the war in Vietnam, which was still fairly remote for most Tuskegee people, but which was drawing closer every day. On January 6, 1966, SNCC had made its first official statement against American aggression in Vietnam and American foreign policy generally. SNCC had been preparing to issue such a statement for months; the murder of Sammy Younge was the catalyst that prompted the organization to do so:

> The murder of Samuel Younge in Tuskegee, Alabama, is no different than the murder of peasants in Vietnam, for both Younge and the Vietnamese sought—and are seeking—to secure the rights guaranteed them by law. In each case, the United States bears a great part of the responsibility for these deaths. Samuel Younge was murdered because U.S. law is not being enforced. Vietnamese are murdered because the United States is pursuing an aggressive policy in violation of international law. The United States is no respecter of persons or law when such persons or laws run counter to its needs and desires.

SNCC saw a clear relationship between racism and the Vietnam war, but at that time many people—black as well as white—refused to see the connection. This national issue also divided the Tuskegee Institute campus.

GWEN PATTON: There seemed to be a real great conflict about the war. Simuel Schutz, Betty Shields, and other people were concerned about the war; they felt that there was a connection between the war and civil rights. And

there were others who were not really concerned about the
war, who felt that the two issues should be separated. That
helped to disintegrate TIAL too.

The war and the draft would become issues of growing importance on the Tuskegee campus. Simuel Schutz,
for one, became directly involved. He was sent a notice to
report for a preinduction physical on May 4, 1966, but
didn't receive it until the day itself because he was out in
Lowndes County getting people to the polls to vote in the
primary election of May 3. He reported to his draft board
one day late. The FBI was on hand, somehow, and Schutz
confirmed to the agent that he did not intend to go into
the Army. Schutz was later indicted and, that fall, sentenced in the same Opelika courthouse where Segrest had
gone free. The sentence: three years in jail for being one
day late. But in the spring of 1966, neither Schutz nor anyone else could generate much support on the draft issue at
Tuskegee. ROTC was still a big thing on campus, and even
within TIAL, numerous young blacks were not yet ready
to reject the military.

Meanwhile, the Ad Hoc Committee for Justice continued to knock on the doors downtown—sharply and per-
sistently, but without success. The kinds of frustration experienced by the Committee are suggested in its report of
March 26, 1966, on the Macon County Board of Revenue.
The Committee had posed many questions to the Board.
Here are two sample questions and the Board's answers:

> Q: Why is the greater part of the Board's public funds
> kept in the Tuskegee Bank, controlled by E. C.
> Laslie, Chairman of the Board? Is there a conflict of
> interest here?

A: All the Bank does is serve as a depository for holding money. There can certainly be no conflict of
interest in that.

Q: How did the Board incur an expenditure of $11,183
labeled "miscellaneous" during six months of operation in 1965?

A: There are several standard items that are miscellaneous.

Bald-faced denials of reality and bland evasiveness:
such was the style of the white power structure in Tuskegee. But the winds of change were slowly blowing across
the South. In 1965, thousands of black people had registered
to vote; the possibility of electing blacks to office in many
places became real for the first time since Reconstruction.
In Macon County, several thousand black people—particularly in rural areas—had been added to the voting rolls,
thanks to the efforts of young people like Sammy Younge.
Now the spring primaries were coming up in preparation
for the November, 1966, elections. The Lowndes County
Freedom Organization was running a slate of candidates
for local offices, under its black panther symbol.

Lucius Amerson, a black man, decided that the time
had come for him to run for sheriff of Macon County in
the May 3 primary of the Democratic Party. Although he
didn't say so at the time, Amerson must have felt that the
murder of Sammy Younge was an additional, important
factor in creating a favorable climate for his candidacy.

Amerson, then thirty-two years old, was an Army
veteran of eight years' service who had been a paratrooper
on active duty as well as a military instructor. While in
the service, he had taken courses in methods of law enforcement and later studied criminology and social science
at Tuskegee Institute. He had worked in food service at

the Veterans' Administration Hospital in Tuskegee and as a postal clerk ("A good job for a Negro," they said in Alabama).

The office of sheriff was a position which carried power not only in matters of law enforcement and many aspects of daily life (such as the liquor traffic), but also on the personal, financial level. In Alabama, sheriffs do not receive a fixed salary but fees and fines ($3.00 per arrest, for example). By this method, it has been estimated, a sheriff can earn as much as $25,000 a year. The idea of a black man in Alabama having such powers, and making that kind of money, made a lot of people very nervous.

Amerson never presented himself as a "Black Power" candidate in campaigning for the primary. But he was still opposed by the Negro leadership—particularly the TCA and its political arm, the Macon County Democratic Club. One must recall that, in the 1964 elections, those groups had sought to reassure whites by trying only to desegregate rather than to control city and local government. Although blacks finally held a voting majority, they had put brothers into only two out of the five City Council seats in Tuskegee; only one brother into the four elective positions on the Macon County Commission; only two blacks into the five seats on the Macon County School Board. In 1966, Dean Gomillion, who was both head of the TCA and president of the Macon County Democratic Club, had still not moved from that go-slow position. Aside from the fact that this leadership may really have been worried about what would happen if they did not appease the whites, they certainly also had a desire to maintain control and a fear of losing power to the upcoming, younger blacks.

But the young bloods had no intention of lying down and letting TCA run the show again. As the May 3 primary approached, the TIAL students decided to lend their support to Amerson and other black candidates.

SCOTT B. SMITH: Amerson made appeals to students indirectly. He didn't appeal to activist students but to others. He said he wasn't for Black Power, that he was in the Democratic Party. He would ask students who had cars to go out in the community.

GWEN PATTON: The students sought to support Amerson as TIAL members and as a TIAL group, but he didn't want our support as a group and he told us that. But he sought out individuals to help him. For instance, he asked me, Tippy, and Wendy if we would help him in his campaign. But we acted as individuals, not as a group. We would go campaigning with him through the county. We organized a rally for him downtown. We got some students off-campus to play their instruments and have a dance downtown. What we were saying in this campaign was, "Vote for Amerson—he would make the best sheriff, he is qualified, he has more education than the other candidates"—that kind of thing.

Amerson won enough votes in the primary to enter a runoff election against the incumbent white sheriff. In the period between the primary and the runoff, which was scheduled for May 31, there were some new factors in the political climate of Tuskegee. For one thing, Mrs. Lurleen Wallace had won a sweeping victory in the race for governor on May 3—which iced any idea that Alabama whites were getting less racist. Secondly, many of the blacks in the primary elections for local offices had been defeated because whites voted along a race line while the black voters often cast their ballots for white as well as black candidates. The lesson of that experience was clear, too. Among the students, a less tangible but certainly influential factor was the election on May 7 of Stokely Carmichael—advocate of "Black Panther" independent politics—as the new chairman of SNCC.

In Macon County itself, there was still another reason for change in the climate: growing disaffection in the black middle class with the established black leadership. Much of this centered on what happened to Arthur Scavella, a black man, who had run in the primary against a white woman for a Board of Education position and lost.

Like Amerson, Scavella was thirty-two years old at that time; he had attended Tuskegee Institute and been president of the Student Government. He had gone on to obtain a Master's Degree from the University of Michigan and then returned to teach at Tuskegee Institute in 1957; later, he became head of the mathematics department.

ARTHUR SCAVELLA: I decided to run basically because I'm aware of the need for improved education in this county. We don't have a good school system and getting a better one depends a great deal on the composition of the Board of Education. The bad conditions in the schools had racial connections, but all the things which motivated me did not. For example, even the school downtown—which did have desegregation (but perhaps not to the extent that it should) —I wouldn't say that's a good school.

Another thing was that the white lady I ran against, Mrs. Frances Rush, was supposed to be a liberal, but I was at a meeting in one of the churches here where she was the speaker and she spoke too much like a Southerner for me. She didn't sound liberal to me and she didn't sound liberal to most of my close friends here. Had I not opposed her, probably no one would have.

The major problem I confronted in my campaign was that I did not get the support of the Negro leadership here in Tuskegee. As it turned out, I didn't lose but by about three hundred votes. I lost out in rural areas like Shorter—I'm sure primarily because the leaders there were persuaded by the Negro leadership in Tuskegee. But it wouldn't be fair to say the rural people in general voted like that, because my best margin came in the rural precinct of the Fort Davis area. That can be attributed primarily to the fact that the Negro leadership there was not persuaded by the dictates of the Tuskegee Negroes and tended to be independent of the Montgomery Association. Out in Fort Davis, the leader just said he knew everybody out there wanted me. That was primarily because I'd gone out there and given a speech at the church along with the other candidates. They thought a lot of me and invited me back.

There were a number of Tuskegee leaders for me, but those that counted the most were not for me. They didn't read my name [from the list of those supported by "the leaders"] except, I guess, out in Fort Davis. The list . . . that's what I mean when I say I did not have the support of the Negro leaders. That was the way they made their support manifest—in addition to any talking they might have done in their little Democratic Club meetings. In order for me to win, I had to be on the list. But I didn't mind working against the odds.

The Negro leadership was opposed to me for several reasons. One had to be that they seemed to feel my opponent represented an important element of the white community. And they also felt that her defeat might result in a breakdown of whatever good relations might have existed between the races. It was part of the general feeling that, although Negroes are in the vast majority, it would not be wise for Negroes to dominate any of the major bodies—the Board of Education being one of them. They have a plan which to many of us doesn't make sense, a plan based upon gradualism, the feeling being that if it were not done that way then it would become an all-black community—which that group opposes. In other words, desegregation and eventual integration is their major hope. And so they didn't want a Negro sheriff either, and one got the impression during the campaign that sheriff was certainly one position that wouldn't be won by a Negro. There was a lot of talk about how a Negro sheriff just couldn't do the job here, that he'd probably be shot.

But there are many of us who feel that, well, goodness, we are the vast majority here; we have the economic resources, we have the education, and we are best qualified to run the affairs of the county and the town. This is the way more and more Negroes feel about it every day. There has to be something of a break in the power. Of course, the leadership is getting older and older. I sort of look at them as a parallel to the Dixiecrats. All these guys will, in time, be swept aside by the course of history.*

Mrs. Washington, Laly's mother and a prominent member of the Tuskegee middle-income group, was one of those who supported Scavella in defiance of the TCA. Her comments on the election revealed the split that had

* Speaking of history, it is interesting to note that the black woman who ran for the School Board twelve years before Scavella (see Chapter II) was defeated by a margin of votes almost exactly matching the numerical difference between black and white voters in Macon County. Apparently, black Tuskegee had no hang-ups about voting in a bloc then; that came later.

developed in the middle class over the established leadership.

MRS. WASHINGTON: The first year we had the majority vote, in 1964, I felt we owed it to Dean Gomillion to vote like he told us. And I told him that, too. I said, "You have fought to get us to this point and I'm going to follow you and I'm going to try to persuade everybody I know to vote as you say. This is a respect vote and a thank-you vote. But after this one, it is every man for himself." So I held my nose and voted for Bull Connor for Democratic National Committeeman. He told me that I didn't *have* to vote for Bull Connor, he didn't ask anybody to vote against his conscience. I just really felt that, the first time around, Dean Gomillion was due a community vote of appreciation.

Now, Mr. Scavella was really a candidate worthy of support. He's a sensible person but he's not an Uncle Tom. He feels sympathetic with the young people—he doesn't reject them because he thinks they are screwball. He had been selected teacher of the year two times in the last five years. He had involved himself in volunteer activities, and he is intensely interested in upgrading the curriculum offered in the schools for Negro children. He has been invited by the state curriculum committee to go to these meetings to set up a curriculum for state schools. He is very articulate and a very forceful speaker. And he convinced the rural people—they just loved him. His name gave them some problems—they called him Novella, Avella, anything but what it was, but they knew who he was and they really responded to him. The woman he was running against didn't even have a college degree. There was just no comparison . . . this was a clear-cut case.

I encouraged Mr. Scavella to run, I just about insisted

that somebody oppose Mrs. Rush. I insisted that he go to
see Dean Gomillion and tell him that he was planning to
run and find out if there were any persons that the TCA
had already selected to support, because we didn't want
to pull the Negro vote apart. Gomillion told Mr. Scavella
that any eligible citizen had the privilege of running for
office.

Later, I told Gomillion that I was going to support
Mr. Scavella and I asked him if he and his organization
would support him. And Gomillion told me that his organization didn't endorse candidates. I told him that if he
was not for Mr. Scavella, then he was my enemy and I
would fight him with everything I could. There was nothing underhanded about my dealings with Gomillion. I
didn't want to have to be deceitful about it.

I'm the financial secretary of the Macon County
Democratic Club—I'm supposed to be in the power structure. But once I had declared myself in opposition to them,
I never got any more notices of meetings. I thought that if
Dean Gomillion wasn't going to support Scavella, he should
have said so. But he implied that he was going to leave this
thing alone and let every candidate get out and drum up
his own trade.

That's what I'm mad about—not about his losing. I
told Gomillion after the election, "I'm not mad because we
lost, I'm disappointed. But I'm mad at the *way* we lost. I'm
mad about that list. You told me that your organization
didn't endorse candidates and I reminded you of the list.
And you told me that it was not going to be your policy to
endorse candidates. I don't intend for that to happen again,"
I told him. "I'm going to be very active." He said, "Oh,
don't leave us." I said, "I have no intentions of leaving. I'm
going to stay right in here and fight you." I wasn't really
mad at him because I like Dean Gomillion. I can't help but

admire him for what he has done through the years. But it seems to me that our best bet in this community is to get some new leaders.

I dare say that eighty per cent of the members of the TCA voted for Scavella. But they didn't go to the meetings. After the election, we started drumming up crowds and we had full houses. It used to be ten or eleven people at these little old dry meetings. But they aren't dry any more. Seven or eight hands are going to go up with questions after somebody speaks.

At one TCA meeting, I asked how the beat leaders—they're like precinct leaders—were selected. "They are elected by the people in the precinct," was Dean Gomillion's answer. I said, "Well, I don't ever recall having been asked to come to a meeting to vote on Mr. Sylvester Harris, who is our leader."

Then I met Mr. Harris in the post office and I said, "How did you get to be my leader?"

He said, "Oh, Dean Gomillion appointed me."

So I told Dean Gomillion, "You know, I think there is something wrong because Mr. Harris himself is not even aware of the fact that he was elected. He told me that you had asked him to serve."

Dean Gomillion said, "Well, he's just confused."

And I said, "Now what kind of a leader is that, when he doesn't even know how he got to be our leader?" Then I asked, "What I want to know is, when is the next election?"

He said, "Oh, we will be having one soon."

"Well, when?" I said. "I am grossly interested." I kept asking when the election was going to be, and how it would be publicized. "We really intend to have a representative group out there to elect our next leader," I told him.

"That's fine," Dean Gomillion said, "that's what you

ought to do." I wasn't mad at him, I like him—but liking
and politics are two different things.

We told Scavella afterwards, "We lost in one respect
but we've done this community a service." Had he won,
this community would have been in the same old rutty pattern. I would have, too. His winning would have had an
effect of course, because it would have broken the pattern
of the black vote. But I don't think that it would have
stirred up the community as much, and I think this is
where the stirring up needs to be.

Apparently, Amerson had also been stirred up by the
TCA's position during the primary. There he was, running
against a white man named Harvey Sadler whose qualifica-
tions were that he had run a country store and was the
county's distributor of Sinclair Oil products. Yet the TCA
continued to oppose Amerson as the runoff approached,
with Gomillion stating publicly that he was opposed to
any Southern county having a black sheriff. Amerson
sensed where the people were at, and altered his campaign
style.

GWEN PATTON: He started going around—and I was in
the car—saying that black people ought to stick together,
that black people ought to have a black sheriff, that it's
time now to stop police brutality and that the white man
is not going to do that, that we have to have a black man.
He was a Black Power candidate in a sense; yet, he
wouldn't exactly say that he was for Black Power. During
that time, Black Power wasn't a slogan but the whole ideology of Black Power was in existence. Of course, while he
was talking about black people and using me and Wendy
and Tippy to put across his ideology, he called in SCLC

people to help with his campaign as an organization. SCLC was the organization that was backing him up, which at that time had a very integrated staff.

Two days before the runoff, Reverend K. L. Buford—Vice-President of the TCA and a City Councilman—endorsed Harvey Sadler on the grounds that interracial harmony could not be developed if Negroes "kick white moderates in the teeth." But the tide was running against the old guard. At the last minute, the day before the election, the TCA gave Amerson its blessing. Amerson defeated Sadler by a vote of 3,497 to 3,113. The Democratic nomination assured him of victory in November. Two other black candidates also won offices: L. A. Locklair as tax collector and Harold Webb as member of the County Governing Commission. But they were elderly, light-skinned Negroes; it was the young, dark-skinned Amerson whose victory represented a break with some of Tuskegee's old values.

When I talked with Amerson, he would not allow any record to be made of our conversation. But I remember very clearly his statement that the murder of Sammy Younge had unquestionably helped him to get elected. Some of the middle class was beginning to come back home. It was Sammy Younge, as much as any single person or circumstance, who had opened the way for them. As Scott B. Smith said, "People are looking behind the shining mirror." There would be more for them to see in the year 1966, and they still had a long way to go.

XIV *Justice in Opelika*

The death of Sammy Younge and the life of Lucius Amerson crossed paths in history once again that year. On Tuesday, November 8, the Democratic slate was swept into office with ease. Harvey Sadler, who had become a write-in candidate for sheriff, picked up only two thousand votes to almost four thousand for Amerson. (The victorious black candidate would not, however, take office until January, 1967.) Two other black candidates, Harold Webb and L. A. Locklair, also won their respective posts; Mrs. Frances Rush, Arthur Scavella's former opponent, ran and won uncontested. Meanwhile, three days before the election—but kept secret until afterward—a decision was made which effectively guaranteed injustice in the Sammy Younge murder case.

Marvin Segrest, the killer of Sammy Younge, had finally been indicted for second-degree murder by the grand jury of Macon County. Segrest's attorneys asked for a change of venue on the grounds that their client could not get "a fair trial" in Macon County. A week before Election Day, a forty-minute hearing on this request was held in Tuskegee. Mary Ellen Gale, a reporter for *The Southern Courier*, was one of those who attended the hearing.

MARY ELLEN GALE: The change of venue hearing—they just sneaked it in in the middle of other business at about four-thirty in the afternoon. The defense brought a lot of witnesses to the stand—city cops and so forth—to testify that Segrest couldn't get a fair trial in Macon County because of all the excitement over Sammy's murder. District

Attorney Tom Young, the prosecutor,* said he thought he could. But he didn't bring any witnesses up to say so. Nobody from the TCA or the Institute, nobody. He asked a few questions, but none of them was germane. For instance, Young asked, "Don't you think all our problems in Macon County would be solved if we could get rid of these SNCC people?" Now, what relevance does that have to the question of changing venue? And then he answered his own question, "I think so." Also, the judge was clearly partial to a change of venue.

Activity by "professional agitators" was emphasized as the main reason why strong protest and resentment had developed over Sammy Younge's murder. Among those called as witnesses to this were Harvey Sadler, still in office as sheriff, and Alton B. Taylor, the director of Public Safety, whose dismissal had been a key demand of the Ad Hoc Committee for Justice. They described the protest marches after Sammy's murder and other student demonstrations. "The defendant cannot have a fair and impartial trial in Macon County," said Segrest's attorneys. But, as a *Southern Courier* editorial stated: "Everyone in the courtroom and the county knew that the real objection was that Macon County's jury list is two-thirds Negro. What the attorneys were really saying is that no white man accused of killing a Negro should have to face a jury of independent Negroes."

On November 12, Judge L. J. Tyner of the Circuit

---

* It was hoped that Attorney General Richmond Flowers would be named prosecutor, but apparently he declined because of his failure to convict in the case of Mrs. Viola Liuzzo's murder.

Court ruled on the motion for a change of venue—but his ruling was not revealed until the day after elections, for reasons not hard to understand. His decision: Segrest could not get a fair trial in Macon County. He would be tried in Lee County, which was only about thirty per cent black and where only a few black people had ever served on state juries. This ruling, which could not be legally appealed, almost guaranteed Segrest an all-white jury.

A federal suit was filed soon afterward (by Montgomery attorney Solomon Seay) charging that the Lee County jury system excluded black people and also discriminated against poor whites. With a hearing on this suit scheduled for December 20, the crackers moved fast. Previously, Segrest's trial had been put off for months on end: now it was scheduled to begin almost immediately, on December 7. The trial would take place in Opelika—the town where Sammy Younge had been jailed in August, 1965. The Man's "justice" can move fast when he wants it to, and in ironic ways.

At that time, SNCC was having one of its biannual meetings of the entire staff in New York State. When I was finally reached at the meeting—by Eldridge Burns and Wendy Paris—the two-day trial had ended. I was therefore not present to witness one of the games Southerners play. But there were many who did.

MARY ELLEN GALE: There were seventy-five candidates for the jury, five of them Negro. In the South, juries are chosen differently from other places—the defense gets to strike two and the prosecution gets to strike one. All the Negroes were struck—by the defense. The jurors chosen were mostly county farmers, small businessmen. They showed up in short-sleeved shirts or T-shirts, no ties.

GWEN PATTON: The defense got the type of jury it

wanted: twelve lily-white, country-bred crackers. That's what Segrest had as a jury. During the trial, some of them went to sleep. There was one tall, redneck cat—I don't think he ever listened to what was happening at all. Tom Young was the prosecutor. He's a white segregationist as far as I'm concerned and he had no intention of trying to win that trial. He called the whites "Mr." and the Negroes by their first names.

The first day of the trial, there were seven students. I couldn't understand that at all when three thousand had marched the day Sammy got killed. I felt that the whole trial should have been packed with black students from Tuskegee and black people from the community. President Foster was not at that trial. Dean Phillips was not at that trial. In fact, no dignitaries from the Institute came.

On the first day, the state presented its witnesses: they included the state toxicologist, a number of black students (particularly Joseph Morris) who had been in two cars parked near the gas station on the night of the shooting, and the white driver of the Atlanta-bound Greyhound bus, W. B. Powell. Some of the testimony, particularly that of the bus driver, was contradictory in detail, but it all added up to a clear case against Segrest. The witnesses confirmed that Sammy had been shot in the head by a bullet from Segrest's gun (shell casings had been found at the station); that Sammy had been running (or "walking") away from Segrest toward the cab stand when the fatal shot was fired; that Segrest fired at Sammy twice. In cross-examination, the defense attorneys concentrated on the black students.

GWEN PATTON: They kept insulting this young man,

who was from Florida. For instance, they asked him, "You're sure Sammy didn't use any curse words with Segrest?" "You're sure he didn't use the word 'mother-fucker,' you're sure he didn't say that?" He got as much foul language into the record as he could. The boy kept answering, "I don't know what Sammy said. All I know is they were in an argument." Raymon said, "Well, there must have been a lot going on that you didn't hear." And the boy said, "That's right—I was watching the gun."

In general, Raymon projected an attitude that these Negro students were lying. He didn't *say* that but he's a good actor. He played it for all it was worth—this poor old man and that young monster.

On the second morning of the trial, December 8, the prosecution continued to present its case briefly and then rested. Among the students present in the white-pillared County Courthouse, the mood of apprehension and help-lessness was rising. Some of the students took out their anger by challenging the segregation of the courthouse restrooms.

GWEN PATTON: The second day there were about fifteen or sixteen more students, which was encouraging. Some of the students who went had never been active in TIAL. Students were very upset. For instance, one guy told a white woman sitting right in front of me, "How come a devil's food cake has to be black and how come an angel-food cake has to be white?" She didn't answer. She moved her seat. Maggie Magee was there, and Laly Washington. Wendy Paris was very upset. He knew what was going to happen but he was trying to be very cool about it. Eldridge Burns was restless. He kept walking up and down and carrying on. I guess I was restless too. I knew what was going to happen, but at the same time I didn't know what was going to happen.

MAGGIE MAGEE: I saw Laly Washington and she seemed upset so I sat down beside her on the bench. She had a cup of coffee from the concession stand. She said that the man at the concession had told her that she couldn't go in a door on that same floor marked "Ladies." So we went over to the man and I asked him, "Where's my rest-room?" I'm white so he said, "You can use that door over there." Then Laly said, "Where's mine?" She had already found out it was down in the basement. He told her, "You're trying to get me—we're not allowed to segregate in here." We went through that process again and after a while, he wouldn't answer—he'd just say, "We're not allowed to segregate in here."

GWEN PATTON: Several girls had asked to use the rest-room—I was one of them. And the man told us to go downstairs, which we did, and then they told us to go outdoors and then down some more stairs. It was marked "Women" instead of "Ladies." So we went back upstairs. Pretty soon there was this constant traffic of Negro students going to the white restroom all the time, going to the restroom, going to the restroom. And we wrote in there: BLACK POWER.

At about 11:00 A.M. that day, the defense began to present its case. It offered as witnesses Marvin Segrest, several blacks who testified that Sammy had harassed Segrest over a long period of time, and sixteen character witnesses for Segrest.

MARY ELLEN GALE: Segrest testified for about one-and-a-half hours, then they broke for lunch. He said that Sammy had given him trouble in the past, tried to run him over with his car. Young did object to this, but was consistently overruled. The Judge would say, "Well, we'll let the argument go a little bit further to see if it's permissible or not." Meanwhile, the jury heard these things. Then the defense produced two Negro fellows who worked part-time at the station to prove that Sammy Younge had tried to run over Segrest. They were shaking so hard that the Judge gave them a handkerchief.

GWEN PATTON: Segrest said he was constantly harassed, year in and year out, by this young man. Didn't know what to do . . . and he didn't intend . . . he even admitted that he killed Sammy. But it wasn't done intentionally and he didn't even know Sammy was dead until 10:00 A.M. the next day. He only wanted to keep the boy from heckling him and harassing him. It was just this real pitiful thing about this old man, this God-fearin' Christian. That whole bit.

MARY ELLEN GALE: Segrest testified that he told Younge to use the regular men's room behind the station, outside. Later he said there were two outside bathrooms and one inside. Yet he claimed there was no segregation at all. And he was never called on that. Young cross-examined him for about five minutes. He didn't ask any of the questions he should have.

Another thing—Segrest said that he was alone at the station except for his wife, who was sleeping in a car behind the station. Which of course brought out that old specter—Sammy was going to rape this poor lady, and

Segrest was trying to imply that he had been afraid for his wife. They called her to the stand, this old chick— it was corny as hell, and irrelevant, but it raised that specter in the minds of those illiterate people on the jury.

Sergeant Prince, the Negro cop, and others tried to establish that the bullet which killed Sammy was a third bullet, fired by somebody else. But they couldn't produce that bullet. Prince was also one of the sixteen character witnesses they produced. You know how that goes—they ask how long did you know the man, twenty-five years or whatever. "Did he have a good reputation?" And the person says yes. "Thank you very much. Good-bye." These witnesses were sharecroppers and poor people from Shorter, about half of them black.

GWEN PATTON: There was this one black cat from the county who came up to the stand, and the defense attorney asked him how long he had known Mr. Segrest. And he named so many years, like "I've been knowing Mr. Segrest for thirty-five years." "Well, how long has Mr. Segrest been a good man?" "Well, he's been a good man for thirty-four years." And everybody really cracked up over that, because he really didn't understand the significance of what he was saying. It was like, you know—Segrest wasn't a good cat anymore 'cause he had killed Sammy.

The total testimony of prosecution and defense was summarized by *The Southern Courier* in its weekend issue of December 17–18 as follows:*

---

* Following the trial, I made several attempts to obtain the full transcript. This effort was finally abandoned because of the lack of local cooperation, the high cost of the transcript, and the fact that the *Courier*'s account was considered accurate by various persons present at the trial.

Segrest said Younge drove his car up to the service station, on Highway 29 just east of Tuskegee, shortly before midnight. He "jumped out cursing and ranting and raving," Segrest said.

When Younge asked where the restroom was, Segrest said he pointed—"ladies on this side, men on this side." When Younge said he wouldn't use a segregated restroom, Segrest said he told Younge, "The only segregation is between men and ladies."

Segrest said Younge replied, " 'I don't go to the goddam back for nobody. The sooner you goddam white folks know I don't go to the back, the better it will be for you.'

". . . I said, 'You just came here to raise hell. Go, and don't come back,' " Segrest testified. He said Younge got back in his car and drove to the Greyhound bus station next door.

"I went back inside," Segrest said. "Then I heard this terrible commotion . . . I went back out. I saw him. He was beyond himself—cursing. . . . He started advancing toward me with this lead pipe or whatever it was . . . I pulled the gun to rout—bluff him, and shot at the blacktop near his feet."

Segrest's testimony on this point conflicted with that of the student witnesses. Radley said that when Younge asked to use the public restroom, Segrest "immediately pulled a gun." Radley, Morris, and Brooks [students] said Segrest pointed the gun at Younge while ordering him to leave the service station.

Segrest said that after he fired the first shot, Younge retreated around the bus parked at the bus station. Then, Segrest said, Younge started back. "He was comin' toward me when I fired the last time," the defendant said. . . . He testified that he shot twice as Younge came toward him, "with something that looked to me like a gun."

But Joseph David Morris, Jr., a Tuskegee Institute student, testified that Segrest fired the second shot as Young was running away. W. B. Powell, the bus driver, said Younge was walking away from Segrest into an alley when the shot was fired. . . .

Both [Segrest and Powell] said Younge walked away from the [second] shot alive. But Morris said that he saw Segrest fire and Younge fall. "I waited a minute or two and pulled [my car] out on the highway with my lights on. I saw him laying in blood on his back. Blood was running down the pavement."

Segrest said he aimed the gun high, over Younge's head. Powell, the bus driver, said Segrest waited to shoot until Younge was "completely out of his line of fire." But Morris said Segrest held the gun level and fired at Younge. . . .

Sergeant George O. Prince, of the Tuskegee police, testified that he was called to the downtown service station where Segrest worked a few minutes before midnight, Jan. 3. Prince said Segrest complained about Younge's behavior. But the policeman didn't remember Segrest saying that Younge had any weapon.

Yet the golf club which police found under Younge's body played a major role in Segrest's testimony in court . . . [Segrest] said the golf club must have been the gun-like "something" he saw in Younge's hands.

In their final arguments, the state attorneys maintained that Segrest had shot Younge and that "there is no legal justification for this killing." District Attorney Young added that the state witnesses had placed Younge too far away from Segrest for a plea of self-defense. "I've never seen any kind of golf stick that has the range of a .38 pistol," he said. But he concluded by saying to the jury, *"All I ask is a verdict that you can sleep with. A verdict that you can walk down any street in this county and never need deny."* With that jury, and in that county, this could mean only one thing.

The defense maintained that "there is a reasonable

doubt about when the boy was killed or who killed him," and that "the defendant had a legal right to protect himself." It also cited differences between the testimony of the bus driver and the students, to strengthen its case. The killing, said Raymon, "should be ruled an unfortunate accident."

Between 4:00 and 5:00 P.M., arguments ended and the Judge gave his instructions to the jury.

GWEN PATTON: The jury went into chambers to make its decision. Well, all of us had gotten restless at the time, and we knew what to expect. But still, we were saying, maybe it won't happen to Sammy, because Sammy was, you know, it just won't happen to Sammy.

The jury was out for an hour and ten minutes, and during that time there was some harassment by us against the white people. We hit people, poked them in the shoulders, 'cause we knew what the verdict was going to be. We had to let out some revenge. We raised all kinds of constitutional questions, and we talked to Tom Young. I got up to go get a drink of water from the lawyers' table. Wendy went out of his mind, came up there, grabbed me and told me I shouldn't have done that. "You know, Gwen, you aren't supposed to drink their water." I wasn't thinking. I said, "Well, fuck it. I don't care."

I wanted some action. I wanted a riot. I wanted to riot right there in the courthouse. And I felt that if we had had enough black people there we could have had a riot. And what was pretty about the whole thing was that a lot of community people had started coming to that trial, a lot of old county people were there. And everytime we looked back, they'd shake their heads at us as though they agreed with what we were trying to do and what we were trying to accomplish. And these people were from Lee County, I would assume, because I had never seen them in Montgomery or in Macon County.

Eldridge went up and talked to Young. I don't know the words they exchanged, but when Young came over to where we were, I got up to meet him halfway and I shook his hand. I said, "Nice case, Mr. Young. Very nice case. You think we're going to win?" And he said something like, "Well, I don't know. You know how it is. You know I just can't say right now." And I was really mad. Like I wanted to spit in his face. I think Wendy was rather upset, but he didn't do anything. He just sat there.

The jury came back, and the same redneck man who slept all the time gave the verdict. And he said, "Not Guilty." I screamed. I said, "God damn!" Just like that. I got up to walk out, and then the Judge said, "Lady, you can't walk out of here until I've said . . ." until he dismissed the court. I looked at him. I said, "I'm fixing to go."

MAGGIE MAGEE: I thought, here it comes. You have to picture the courtroom—the front of it all filled with white lawyers and white officers, talking to one another—they were all at home in that courtroom. And the center section filled with Tuskegee students. I expected Gwen to be dragged out by about twelve officers.

GWEN PATTON: I looked at the Judge and said, "I'm fixing to go." I looked at the other people and I said, "I'm fixing to go. I'm leaving." And I got up and walked on out. Two policemen went to the door to block me, and I said "I got to go." Then Eldridge and Wendy jumped up. Then the other students jumped up and we all walked outside.

MAGGIE MAGEE: Wendy said, "Come on, we're not going to jail in Opelika," and everybody went to their cars. You knew it was the verdict that was coming, so . . . but people were saying, "There's going to be hell to pay in Alabama."

XV   Black Fury Ridin' High

The trial of the nice old white gentleman, one Marvin Segrest, was not a trial to test his guilt but one to test the right of any black man in this country to keep his own life if any white man desires to take it away. Ponder that for a second and then let us move on to this. No white man has ever, in the legal history of this country, been tried, convicted, and executed for the murder of any black man, woman, or child. . . . Sammy Younge's offense on that evening of January 3, 1966, was that he was black and yet wished to urinate in that bathroom clearly designed for white folks. Let us ask ourselves seriously, is it against the law for white folks to kill niggers in this country? Is it really, or are we being duped? And when we begin to suspect the latter, how should we react? Is it society, or more specifically white society, that decides we should react in a way that they would consider imponderable if the situation is reversed?

To be forced to the position of accepting our own genocide because we dare not think independently of white sanctions is to be refused our manhood. . . . What price must we pay for our white-endorsed dignity? . . . We black people are denied even the right to hate openly. My black brother is dead by the hand of one who is not my brother or my friend—have I the right to hate his very guts?

Let us examine the cold precision with which every white man who kills a black man is brought speedily to "justice." Let us note from our examination that there is something amiss. Let us conclude from our notation that this must be ended. . . . Let us then open our minds and create our own system based upon the elimination of white oppression at any cost. If we must die, let us die as men and women.

Ernest Stephens in *Black Thesis*
Tuskegee Institute, December 10, 1966

GWEN PATTON: After the trial, the students rushed back
to Tuskegee. A couple of students wrote a leaflet about
what had happened at the trial and about the verdict,
hoping that this would arouse some type of activity on
campus. We planned a meeting in Logan Hall for about
ten, ten-thirty. There were about three hundred students
at the meeting.

Student leaders were talking. One student got up
and talked about a series of night marches to the homes
of the white jurors. I didn't think that made too much
sense. Another student got up and said that we should
march tomorrow morning at nine. That was George
Davis. That didn't make sense either 'cause the crisis was
now, not at nine in the morning. With people going home
to sleep over it, they might not feel like marching tomorrow morning. It seemed like people should move
now. Sammy's murderer had been acquitted, and we as
black students had to tell Sammy that we didn't dig what
had happened. And we had to do it now. But you couldn't
move with only three hundred people. I didn't know.
. . . I suggested that we adjourn and that the three hundred people go and get Dean Phillips.

SCOTT B. SMITH: The students were very angry, very
frustrated. The girls went to all the dorms, went to the
boys' dorms, everybody's dorm. By midnight, it wasn't
two hundred people. It wasn't three hundred or five
hundred. It was a thousand, fifteen hundred, two thousand.
They were coming in.

GWEN PATTON: Different student leaders got up, and they
talked and they gave their own viewpoint. There was
stuff said about how, when Tuskegee Institute was first

started by Booker T. Washington, he said the school was intended for colored people, and all of a sudden we see white people everywhere we turn. And when the Veterans' Hospital first started out, it was a Negro Veterans' Hospital, and now there're all white people. There are more white people over there in administrative positions than black people. And then there was this whole fever of blackness coming across. Negritude was coming across on students. Students were responding to that, and we correlated that to how Sammy felt. Sammy wasn't concerned about integration, Sammy was trying to do something for his own people and that's what we have to do.

SCOTT B. SMITH: I went to the meeting and told how I felt. "You're not going to lynch Segrest. You're not going to burn his house down. So you got to do something." Then I went downtown to the square with a sleeping bag and waited.

GWEN PATTON: Scott B. said he was going to sleep downtown in front of the Confederate statue—that was the tactic—and he wanted students to meet him there. Then another student, I think it was Carl Fitts, said, "I'm going down there with him! Are you coming with me or are you going to stay here and talk?" Everybody decided we should move then. We should move right then and there. We should go downtown.

We lined up. Then there was this whole hassle about marshals, about who's going to protect who and girls on the inside—that whole bit we learned in '63 about the civil-rights movement. It was discussed that we didn't have to do that. We were going to move down. We weren't going to worry about our own safety. We were just going to demonstrate that we felt this was wrong. We had to do something about it.

Benny James, president of the Student Government, asked for marshals to volunteer. Almost every guy in the auditorium, in the gym, went to the center of the floor. Times before, when you asked for marshals you might have gotten twenty or thirty, but this time we had something like two hundred people coming to the floor volunteering to be a marshal. To be a marshal is a very militant and dangerous thing because he's going to be on the outside. He's the one that's getting the bullet.

There was one girl named Sylvia Phillips who kept saying, "What are we going to do? What are we going to do? Let's do something." Sylvia Phillips is unknown on campus. She's never been to a TIAL meeting. She doesn't know what TIAL is all about, but here she was ready to move and to do something. And there were a lot of other young people who never were members of TIAL, never associated with Sammy—in fact, might not have even known Sammy. But they were ready to move because they could relate what had happened in their lives to what was happening right at that moment.

SCOTT B. SMITH: They said, "Damn the president. Damn the curfew. We're going downtown." And they went.

GWEN PATTON: We had no form, which was beautiful. We had no pattern, which was beautiful. People were just filling the streets, and they weren't singing no freedom songs. They were mad. People would try and strike up a freedom song, but it wouldn't work. All of a sudden you heard this "Black Power, Black Power." People felt what was going on. They were tired of doing this whole

nonviolent bit. They were tired of this organized dem-
onstration-type thing. They were going to do something.

We got to the square. The beautiful thing was that
people who did the talking were mainly black men: black
men were speaking; black men came up with the ideas;
and black men wanted to do something about the whole
situation. The black leaders of the past wanted to have an
all-night vigil. That wasn't what students wanted to do.
They went down there with their minds set on destroying
that city. It was obvious and everybody knew it. We
didn't contact nobody, no professors, and there were no
white people there.

SCOTT B. SMITH: I got the impression they wanted to do
something about the problem, something more than marching, so the statue was it. Wendell and I told them to get
some black paint.

GWEN PATTON: The appeal was made to a community
person, 'cause we thought that would be important. So
out of the clear blue sky, this community man came up
with two cans of black paint.

SCOTT B. SMITH: Where they got black paint that late
at night, I don't know. They got it. They had their guns;
they were ready. They had their little Molotov cocktails
—Listerine bottles, you know, with napkins. Got the girls
to give them some napkins—Tampax, Kotex—putting it
in the bottles. They were ready, man. They were using
things they had learned from ROTC. They were using
these things for offense measures. The question came up
that when we get back from Vietnam, things going to

change. We're not going to take a lot of things that've been going on.

GWEN PATTON: So they painted the statue black and people liked that. They dug that. They painted a yellow stripe down the back of the statue. Then they painted "Black Power" and "Sam Younge" on the base.

SCOTT B. SMITH: When the paint hit, a roar came up from those students. Every time the brush hit, *wham*, they'd roar again. There were brushfires around the statue, dead leaves. There was a girl standing there—not crying, but whimpering. And she said, "Let's get *all* the statues—not just one. Let's go all over the state and get all the statues." She's a very quiet person, but this time she was very angry. We sang "We Ain't Gonna Be Nonviolent" and "Take This Hammer"—the song that goes "Captain called me nappy-headed nigger ain't my name." We couldn't get the students to respond to "We Shall Overcome."

Dean Phillips and the rest of them stood there watching—they couldn't stop the students. The Dean didn't want to stop them at all. Actually, he was tickled pink the way it was going. He was cracking up laughing, when they painted the statue black. That paint wouldn't come off, either—they tried everything.

"Local police circled the square during the demonstration," *The Southern Courier* reported, "Negro patrolmen occasionally came into the square to speak to the students. White patrolmen stayed across the street." This was the students' night.

GWEN PATTON: After they painted the statue, people

wanted to do something else. So everyone said, "Gwen, can we walk? Can we walk around town? What are we going to do? We're not going to stand here all night, are we? Let's move. Let's move." There was this constant thing by the black student leaders to stay where we were, to sit down, to be still, like the old demonstration bit. And students couldn't understand that. And then the *cops* had a tactic. The cops come running over saying, "There's a white man on top of a building with a gun in his hand. He going to shoot into the crowd." Well, this was the tactic they used to make the group panic, to make the group want to disperse. So we went around saying there was no such thing. Ain't no white man on top of the building. How's he going to get on the building? Then the students were pacified.

But after a while, about three o'clock, nothing was happening. People were just sitting there, and they started going back to the campus. That always happens in a demonstration—nothing to do. So the peaceful people left. The angry folks left. Then the angry folks came back —about eight hundred of them.

SCOTT B. SMITH: They wanted someone to tell them to go ahead and tear things up. No, baby, I wasn't about to get caught in that trap. They wanted Gwen or Wendell to say to go ahead and do it. So we said, "Do what the spirit say do."

That's when the rocks got thrown and the fires. They would set things on fire with something dry—old dry leaves. But the Molotov cocktails wouldn't ignite right. They threw some bricks in a church and knocked some windows out in a home. Car tires got slashed. Windows got knocked out in cars. Then they headed back to campus.

Thirteen places of business—every large plate-glass window along a one-block stretch of North Main Street —got it that night. Seven city policemen walked behind the group of some 250 students, and did not interfere. And no state troopers showed their faces.

SCOTT B. SMITH: There was a white guy some students had pulled out of a car on Highway 80. They had him behind the dairy bar. I went back behind the dairy bar, which is right alongside the county jail. They had the guy on the ground and were going to beat his brains in with some bricks. I had to grab him from the students, and I got hit up 'side my head. When he got back in his car, he was so shook that his car engine was going and he was trying to start his car. And they were throwing bricks in his car, trying to get him anyway. They got angry at me 'cause I had pulled him up. There I was trying to pull him up, and they were yelling, "Kill the cracker. Eye for an eye. We'll kill a cracker for Sammy Younge." So I got roughed up—the guy said he was sorry but he'd have done it again 'cause I saved a white man. He didn't like it because I was a black man saving a white man. He said, "We're still tight, but don't do it again."

The sheriff had more than enough time to gather his forces, but they weren't ready. I believe at that time the students would have gone up barehanded against a man with a pistol. The whole thing that came out was an eye for an eye. You hit me, I'm going to hit you back. But now it's changed. I'll hit you first before you hit me back. This is what's going on now.

Some of the community people weren't satisfied, however. "Why didn't you tear up the service station?"

they asked. "Why didn't you tear up the office of that fool lawyer who freed this cracker Segrest?"

All that was early in the morning of Friday, December 9. Within five hours, President L. H. Foster of Tuskegee Institute—who had made no statement on the trial as a miscarriage of justice—was condemning the students' actions.

GWEN PATTON: President Foster had called the student body into Logan Hall to discuss the violence that we had done. We had broken some windows and we had to discuss the violence we had done. He made reference to outside agitators—me and Wendy, you know, 'cause we were the only outside agitators there—me and Wendy, since we had already graduated from school. Foster gave this great speech about how much money we had caused the Institute to put out to pay for the damages. And students were really rallying behind him.

SCOTT B. SMITH: He said that Tuskegee was an educational place, an educational institution. This was no place for students to commit violence and destruction of property. This was no place, also, for civil-rights activity. He pinpointed civil rights.

None of Tuskegee's thirty-odd community organizations issued a statement on the trial, but everyone rushed forward to condemn the student violence. "The wanton destruction of property downtown . . . cannot be excused," editorialized the weekly *Tuskegee News*. "Professional agitators" came in for sharp attack, while little mention was made of the Klan cross burned in front of the all-black Washington Public School that Friday evening. The suit challenging the Lee County jury system was dismissed on December 20, but still the Establishment talked about the need to respect "legal process," law and order. Sheriff-elect Lucius Amerson made a get-acquainted appearance before the Board of Revenue on December 12, and the Board quickly reappointed outgoing Sheriff Harvey Sadler to a two-year term as beer-license inspector—a job which Amerson expected to get because the enforcement of beer regulations falls under the sheriff's duties. Yet Dr. Foster could say, "We must always try to build on the finer possibilities within men . . . a firm, honest, and cooperative approach."

But some of the young people in and around Tuskegee did not intend to have the clock turned back.

SCOTT B. SMITH: After Foster made his speech. Molotov cocktails started being accumulated around Tuskegee. I don't think Foster realized really how he goofed until later when he got the rumor that some kids wanted to kill him. Some people told me a student was on top of one of the buildings with a rifle and was going to pick Foster off when he came out of his home. They got to him and calmed him down, took him off the roof, and got the rifle away from him. Foster was well aware that there were some attempts being made on his life.

GWEN PATTON: Foster organized a civil-rights conference and set up different groups to discuss strategy. In every last one of those meetings, they had their boy; there was a professor or administrator in every last one of those meetings. We were discussing how we could buy the theater downtown, how we were going to open up a book co-op, a coffee co-op, how we could have a Freedom Christmas for Sammy, and how we were going to set up a memorial for Sammy. Foster planned all these kinds of things. Riot control.

I was in the meeting with Wendy, Scott B., and my good boys from Birmingham. There were white people in the meeting. A motion was made by one of the black cats that we couldn't discuss any techniques and strategy as long as we have the enemy in here. But one of the student leaders said that we could discuss anything that we had to say before the public. The boys from Birmingham couldn't say what they had planned before the public. And they kept trying to get the white people out of the meeting.

We started discussing how we could buy some cows and open up this farm co-op. The boys from Birmingham couldn't identify with this because they didn't want to buy no cattle. They didn't understand that whole thing. They raised their hands and said that if they couldn't have certain people leave the room in order for them to discuss their tactics, they were going to leave. So they walked out.

SCOTT B. SMITH: Right after the trial was over, we sent letters demanding that people boycott Segrest's station. Segrest sold his franchise. Then we worked on boycotting the town. The boycott was to last a whole six months, trying to dry the town up. Foster started dropping students who were working on the boycott; they couldn't get back in school. A lot of students, because of grades and turmoil and endless frustrations, couldn't get back in. A lot of the students who had been on demonstrations had to get loans from Davis to stay in school. That way, the school controlled them. Davis would have his list of old TIAL members, student activists on campus, and when you'd go to ask for a loan or a scholarship, he'd give you the run-around.

One of the students was making silencers with a .32 pistol in the machine shop. To me he's beautiful 'cause he says, "How else am I to get back in school? What else could I do? I can't go to Davis and get money, so I had to do something." That's what he has to do.

Though they couldn't get in, the hard-core activists stayed around because they were still angry about what they were going to do. Now they have gone back to their own home cities, but they still carry that idea: "We can get killed, but we did something in Tuskegee. We did hit back."

There's a whole thing about blackness now. Negro History is now on campus. We had an African festival —the response of the students was tremendous. They came up afterward to ask questions about Africa, their heritage, what it symbolized. Students are wearing African robes on campus. African songs—you don't hear Bach no more, or Beethoven, or old religious songs. You hear songs which speak of our heritage. Articles are coming up in the student newspaper about Africa. The Afro hairstyles are beginning to be accepted on campus—girls that wear wigs are being ostracized. And the fellows are wearing their hair Afro. This is where it's at. I think there's a new age. The young Southern Negro ain't going to take that old jive. Too many people killed. That's Black Power!

ELDRIDGE BURNS: That man might have killed Sammy, but he sure didn't kill his spirit. That's what's pushing me and some other kids around here. Sammy lying up there in that casket—I just won't forget it. And I'm not going to let those people down there forget it—that they killed Sammy. I'm in this ROTC crap now and I'll get kicked out of that. They know I don't care about the war in

Vietnam, but they still say that I'm in it. So they'll just have to kick me out. I know that Sammy would have done the same thing, and that's the least I could do for him. 'Cause he gave his life, and I haven't given nothin' but time. He was my man, Sammy. Sammy the Lemon man.

Postscript: Rebellion '68

1968: known around the world as the year of student rebellion, from New York City to Buenos Aires and from Paris to Tokyo. Less recognized is the fact that the flood of uprisings was preceded by waves of violent and non-violent protest at a host of black Southern colleges from the spring of 1967 into the early months of 1968. On such campuses as Texas Southern, Central State (in Ohio), Jackson State, Fisk, and Tennessee State, students fought with guns for educational reforms, for their dignity as blacks, and for survival against racist white cops who occupied their campuses and brutalized their classmates. Five students at Texas Southern University, members of the campus Friends of SNCC, were indicted on a charge of murdering one cop. Unquestioned evidence points to the fact this policeman was killed by a ricocheting bullet. He was hit near a building where there were no windows— a building in which only some of the five accused were located at the time.

In the spring of 1968, four students at South Carolina State College in Orangeburg were viciously fired upon, wounded and killed by state troopers one night during a period when students were attempting to desegregate a local bowling alley. Cleveland Sellers, who rode with me and others from SNCC to the funeral of Sammy Younge, was shot in the back and imprisoned during the Orangeburg Massacre. Upon his release from jail in South Carolina, he was convicted in Atlanta, Georgia, of refusing to serve in the United States Armed forces, and sentenced to five years in jail.

The student movement which had been born on such Southern campuses on February 1, 1960, saw a resurgence of activity in 1968, but in a new spirit of revolutionary militance and concern not for dignity through lunch-counter demonstrations—but for making the "Negro" college a relevant black institution by seizing and holding power. A rising tide of consciousness that we are Africans, an African people living in the United States and faced with the problem of sheer survival, dominates the thoughts of many black college students today. Plagued by the war in Vietnam, rising repression by the police and other governmental agencies, and filled with a desire to implement Black Power for survival, college students have had to become more militant in their techniques of resistance.

The wave of 1968 did not bypass Tuskegee Institute. About a week after students at Howard University occupied campus buildings there, Tuskegee students "liberated" not merely a piece of the physical plant, but one containing the president and the trustees themselves—including General Lucius B. Clay—as a means of pressing their demands. Shortly afterward came the long occupation of Columbia University, where again it was black students who initiated the action.

At many of the schools where student rebellions have taken place, observers expressed amazement: "How did it happen?" There were those who said that about Tuskegee, too. They did not know the story of Sammy Younge and his fellow activists. A straight line can be drawn from Sammy's lifetime to the events of spring, 1968, at Tuskegee and on into a future which remains to be written. The ripples produced by the Montgomery demonstrations of 1965 became a wave three years later. The president of the Student Government Association in 1968, Warren

Hamilton, was one of the students who had been activated
by what happened at the State Capitol. Ernest Stephens
was on hand too, and Scott B. Smith, as was Wendy Paris
and his younger brother, Cecil.

Michael Wright was the black student at the center
of the Tuskegee uprising that spring. He tells the story
of what happened between February and June, 1968:

MICHAEL WRIGHT: In February, we were trying to form
a SNCC chapter on campus. We got a group going but
later it disbanded. Then five of us went to Orangeburg
the day after the students were shot down. We realized
that the same thing could happen at Tuskegee that had
happened in Orangeburg, and we had to protect ourselves.
That's when Unity developed. Some people from Central
State, where they also had a Unity organization, helped
in setting it up. It was designed to present student grievances to the administration.

The first major issue for Unity was my case. Some
representatives of the State Department had been invited
by the administration to speak in the College Union on
February 29th. I and some other students, wanting to
make Tuskegee a black thing—realizing black ideas—decided to have a demonstration and disrupt the program.
This was something unprecedented in Tuskegee's history.
We went up to the podium and said something like, "In-
asmuch as our Vietnamese brothers don't have an air force
adequate to do their bombing, we their black brothers will
help them." And we started throwing eggs.

Smack, plop, drip—there went the Tuskegee image of
propriety and decorum. The reaction of shock and dis-

approval was answered in a statement issued the next day
by Warren Hamilton, who said, among other things:

> Tuskegee's indigenous Uncle Toms and Aunt Tinas
> had one immediate reaction . . . oh my God. . . . Sorry,
> Master Boss, these boys is jus' a little heated up, they
> don't represent Tuskegee's more civilized . . . here, let
> me help you clean off your suit. . . .
>
> We realize that many brothers and sisters don't
> understand just what went down. The simple fact is
> that the involved students, black men, designed and
> executed an assault *on the State Department* in order to
> intimidate, harass, and otherwise bother them. . . . They
> continue coming to black schools to mock the lack of
> political sophistication (by their standards) of black
> people by simply coming down and *lying* . . . the Texas
> Ranger speaks with forked tongue! . . . These students
> went to bring focus on the fact that a brainwashing
> process is being leveled on black students nationwide to
> buy the leadership off and keep the black masses sub-
> missive.
>
> We as black men resolve to carry on the struggle
> for liberation of all oppressed and exploited people.
> . . . Which side are you on?

At Columbia University, a few weeks later, the throwing of a custard pie at a visiting general would help to
break the ice for what became a massive, "undignified"
student revolt. Now, at Tuskegee, the egg-throwing set
off a quick flow of events.

MICHAEL WRIGHT: Within half an hour, the administration lackeys were determining our fate. They began their
judicial procedure. They called the Institute Court, which
would make its referral to the Judicial Review Board. We
challenged the whole judicial procedure and tried to amass

student support. This was when Unity became visible for the first time.

I got them all hung up in procedure, which was my intent in the first place. We went through a series of letters; as it turned out, I got placed on social disciplinary probation for the rest of the semester because the students would not allow me to be kicked out. That silenced me politically during the first part of March.

President Foster called the first of several All-Institute meetings for March 7 to discuss "problems disturbing the students generally," at which he would answer written questions from the floor. Unity threatened a boycott if there wasn't free-flowing dialogue; that was conceded. At the meeting, Foster said there were "no major or unresolved minor problems." He could not have been more wrong.

MICHAEL WRIGHT: On March 11, Stokely spoke in Logan Hall. The students decided that no white press would be allowed at the "Back to Black" performance preceding Stokely or during his lecture. Myself and Johnny Jackson took charge of security and we didn't have too many problems. The major difficulty was with the administration over who was going to run the thing. The president got on TV and apologized for what happened with the press, in order to keep his thing with the state of Alabama.

Unity kept meeting but the president began repressive tactics. He said we couldn't hold meetings on campus. All you're allowed to do at Tuskegee is eat, study, go to the library, go home. But no one obeyed.

On March 19, the "Unity for Unity" group from Central State University called a meeting in the Student Union. The Dean of Students at Tuskegee, Bert Phillips, said it was unauthorized and could not be held. It was held anyway and five more students were placed on social and administrative probation. The next day, another unauthorized meeting was called.

MICHAEL WRIGHT: Some two hundred students appeared. The Dean of Students came and said we couldn't hold the meeting, to which we replied that we'd hold it at the president's house. He was out of town, and during the course of the evening a window got broken. The students were honestly trying to act in good faith at this time and they took up an immediate collection to pay for the window.

Unity got together and presented a statement of demands, including that the students on social disciplinary probation be taken off. Other demands included restoration of the student judicial system, voluntary instead of compulsory ROTC, longer library hours, student representation on policy-making boards, and athletic scholarships. The administration took a look at the demands and there was a lot of bullshitting. Then the students sat-in at the administration building. The president began to look at the issues more realistically. A student-faculty joint committee was set up to make recommendations.

On March 25, there was a student boycott of classes. It was pretty damned effective. The administration met with the committee and responded to proposals. Foster agreed to reinstate the student judicial system and extend library hours. He said that other things, like voluntary ROTC, would have to wait for the Board of Trustees to decide. Students went back to class.

Press coverage of the student boycott was typical. "If a militant minority is allowed to take over," droned a WSFA-TV editorial, "it quickly disrupts the educational opportunities of the peaceful majority. . . . it's time for strong administrative action whenever and wherever restlessness starts changing into recklessness." The same line that students have heard everywhere—but WSFA-TV had seen nothing yet. The engineering students were about to do their thing, too.

In December, 1967, the engineering students had presented a list of fourteen well-documented demands called a mandate. The most controversial of these was that certain teachers whom the students found incompetent and who had repeatedly demonstrated they were unable to "reach the majority of the students" be removed. Nothing had been done since then about the mandate. Now ACASE (the Ad Hoc Committee for the Advancement of the School of Engineering) renewed pressure for a conference on the demands. On March 21, it announced that classes would be boycotted and the School of Engineering picketed.

MICHAEL WRIGHT: The next few days, activity centered around the engineering students. It was on March 27 that they had their boycott, in which they took over the building. Non-engineering students joined the picket lines. Negotiations with the administration went on but at that time they met with no real success. The problem was that the inclusion of those thirteen other demands—on which the administration was willing to make concessions—weakened the main demand that certain teachers be fired. The Administration wouldn't even consider that one.

The Engineering Building remained occupied while the administration called for students to vote in a referendum on closing down the Engineering School for the semester—a referendum whose formulation ACASE condemned as a case of "heads I win, tails you lose." The vote thus came out 7 in favor and 4 against, with 151 no-votes. The engineering students wanted their school to be open, but not on the president's terms. They held their own referendum, formulated differently, and this time the vote was: 99.6% against closing the school, 95% against accepting the adminstration's proposal, 96.8% affirming that the administration had not done its best to resolve the issue of dismissing ineffective teachers.

Then came Founder's Day—April 7—an occasion on which the Board of Trustees and alumni spent a long weekend at Tuskegee. As on the Founder's Day described by Ralph Ellison in *The Invisible Man*, the trustees were mostly white. They included General Lucius B. Clay, former U.S. military governor of Germany; Rep. Frances Bolton, Ohio Republican; Chairman of the Board Basil O'Conner, president of the National Foundation (March of Dimes). But the program would be very different from the one in Ellison's book.

MICHAEL WRIGHT: Some students got together to plan a demonstration in support of our demands. We wanted to show the trustees that all was not well at Tuskegee behind that façade of normalcy. Another object was to get President Foster to confer with the trustees on some of the issues which he had said he could not decide unilaterally. For example, the trustees had to act on the issues of athletic scholarships and making ROTC compulsory only for freshmen—which had finally been recommended by an administration committee.

On April 4, our mandate [the same term that was used by engineers] was prepared. It ran to over twenty pages. Although all the issues up to then centered around the black university concept, we never put them in those terms until that mandate. There were efforts to sabotage it. The mandate had been left in the hands of a committee to have it printed up in the Dean of Students' Office. We found that the committee had reduced it from twenty-two pages to three. A hysterical scene followed because we found this cut at ten o'clock in the morning of the day it was to be presented.

The mandate was given to the trustees when they arrived on Friday, April 5. For the first time, the students' demands included a statement of "general philosophy—a black university concept." It said:

> If Tuskegee cannot learn from and be designed to benefit the black community, then it does not need to exist; to hand America a carbon copy of itself is now archaic, insulting, and irrelevant. We, as black people, need and will have educational institutions that speak from a black experience and address themselves to black collective needs.
> The individual considerations are now secondary to a collective ethos—this is the order of the day!

Specific demands included the addition of courses in Afro-American history and sociology and African languages, as well as a changed emphasis in all social science disciplines which would relate them to the black experience. A new school of Fine Arts was demanded as well as a major in music and the establishment of a student theater which would not be prevented from doing productions that expressed black needs, black ideas, and black talent, as happened with the current Little Theater. The demands of the Tuskegee students were thus basically the same as those of Afro-American students everywhere. The students wanted an education that would be relevant to dealing with the problems they would face after college. This was true of all demands, whether they involved abolishing ROTC or adding a black studies program. "Our era marks the end of the Negro and the beginning of a proud race of people, the Afro-American," the mandate concluded. "We want the Tuskegee Institute student of tomorrow to know and be proud because he is black."

As for the engineers, all of their demands but one—the important one—had been met by now. They pressed the trustees to approve the dismissal of certain teachers, and were rebuffed. Early in the morning of April 6, ACASE issued a statement to all fellow students calling for their support. "The trustees cannot be trusted," it said. But the other students were already on the move.

MICHAEL WRIGHT: That Thursday evening, Dr. King had been shot. That threatened to disrupt our whole plan. But we got together and decided we must continue, because if we changed our plans we would never get them back to that point.

The plan was to stop all activities on campus so that the trustees would have to do some serious thinking about our demands. About twenty to thirty students decided to lock up all the buildings except the cafeteria and snack bar. By Friday morning, April 5, all the academic buildings were locked up. They cut off the locks, we put them on again. Four to five hundred people began marching around campus with picket signs. To divert the administration's attention off Dorothy Hall, where the trustees would be meeting, students began picketing the administration building.

At four-thirty that afternoon, we went in to meet with the trustees. Five minutes later, as planned, we were followed by the Communications Committee. Their job was twofold: to take over the central telephone system and to set up a PA system so that we could be in communication with the students outside the building after we were locked in. There was also the Lock-Up Committee, whose job was to lock up Dorothy Hall. All this was supposed to happen within six minutes. It was timed right down to the minute.

After the building was locked up, President Foster came down and started suspending people. A lot of students got scared and a lot didn't. The Student Ad Hoc Committee was the major student group appearing before the Board of Trustees. It included some pretty backward students and we knew from the beginning that there would be a split. To help balance opinion, however, the Ad Hoc Committee had called upon six resource people, which included myself.

As a result of our action, the trustees said they'd give us a meeting the next day from 11:15 to 12 noon to talk about our mandate. There was enough student support to continue the demonstration so we sneaked in with blankets and food. That night we held some political workshops.

Saturday morning we continued much the same way. While the meeting was starting with the trustees at 11:15, the doors were again locked; the central telephone system was securely taken over, the students ate the lunch prepared for the trustees, and the trustees were unable to leave the building. We negotiated and negotiated with the trustees over our mandate. They presented a proposal but it was not acceptable.

The trustees' reply to the students' mandate was a muddle of self-justification, vagueness, and bureaucratic double-talk. On the black university concept, they had this to say:

> . . . The questions you raise deserve the gravest consideration, and it is our intention to see that this is done over the coming months through the comprehensive study of Tuskegee's future role and scope . . .

MICHAEL WRIGHT: About seven, eight o'clock, that evening, Sheriff Amerson turned up and tried to get in to deliver an injunction against us. No one would let him in. There was also word that the National Guard was being mobilized. We were not prepared to deal with them as we should have been, but at the same time we would not let our thing go. About eight-thirty, nine o'clock, the president read the injunction to the students and also read an order to close the school.

We told the students that the state troopers were on their way, and that the students standing outside should come inside. This was to avoid a situation like that they had had at Orangeburg. A lot of people didn't want to come in so we tried, tried, tried—appealing to them over the microphones. All this time we continued negotiating with the trustees, telling them they could leave if they would consider our demands.

We discussed whether to get President Foster to tell Sheriff Amerson not to bring the state troopers and the National Guard on the campus. They could not come unless they were invited. The decision was placed in the hands of the president and the Board of Trustees. Their response was, "Fuck the students. Let them all get killed —just as long as we get them out of the building." We let the trustees know that whatever happened to us would happen to them.

We were trying to keep the state troopers out and at the same time maintain a bargaining position. To do all this was not the least of the fantastic dilemmas. Community planning was so poor on our part that we couldn't count on them for support. Furthermore, much of our planning had to be done in secret from the students—let alone from the rest of the community. It was an up-tight situation.

Between 12:30 and 1:00 A.M., the trustees made their first attempt to get out but the students wouldn't let them. People then began arguing, "Let them go. They can't do us no more good." A lot of the students were beginning to get leery about keeping them, what with the threat of the National Guard. The Ad Hoc Committee split, as expected, and voted to let them out. So they got out and the whole thing looked very bleak. But the students would not let the president go—they sent him out on the balcony to answer questions. I just wondered whether in one of the next ten minutes he would fall dead from a heart attack.

At something to three o'clock, we were arguing about whether the National Guard was coming. I was arguing that they were. A hundred, hundred and fifty students were packed like sardines in the Hall. I went up to Foster and told him that if he wanted to get out, he'd better tell Amerson to call off the Guard. The president, being by himself, agreed to do so. I went out to find Amerson. Dean Phillips said, "He's not coming; the students chased him away." I couldn't believe that, because a lot of students knew what was happening. I found out that he was the one who had urged Amerson to leave and got students out of the way so Amerson's car could move.

Amerson was to call back in fifteen minutes to find out about the situation. No phone call came. Another half hour went by, no phone call. At about three o'clock in the morning, the National Guard was there. They lined the whole front of the highway and straight to the back of the campus. I've never seen so many Guardsmen! Alabama has the fifth largest contingent of National Guard and state police in the country. There was nothing we could do—we were really in very pitiful shape.

The last of the students then left Dorothy Hall. At that point, according to an April 15 article in the *National Observer*, Major General Taylor Hardin of the Guard told President Foster that his men were ready "to clean troublemakers out of the dormitories." Fortunately Dean Phillips, who had resigned effective at the end of the semester because he couldn't take the pressure from both sides, was still around to protest. The campus was quiet, he said. Guardsmen and administrators then decided that the only remaining point of resistance was the Engineering Building, which had been student-occupied for two weeks. Three to four hundred Guardsmen moved across the campus, "the troops with fixed bayonets," said the *National Observer*. Campus police, who entered first, found nothing except four sleeping students.

Meanwhile, President Luther Foster had made two key moves. He first announced that the entire school would be closed and, somewhat later, that all dormitories absolutely must be vacated by Tuesday, April 9. Even foreign and exchange students were forbidden to remain on campus. With less than forty-eight hours' notice, the telephone lines were jammed with students calling their families. Panic set in; the dormitories were in chaos and the bus station packed as students struggled to meet the deadline. Classes were not to resume for two weeks. In the meantime—and this was the hooker—all students had to file a Statement of Intent in order to be given an application *for readmission to the school!* Not every Statement of Intent would be accepted. And for those accepted, the application for readmission itself required students to sign a statement saying, "It is my firm intention to abide by the rules and regulations of the Institute. . . ."

The purpose of the whole operation was very clear. As Unity said in a statement to the students: "Suppose that all students were out of school, and each student had to apply for readmission. Wouldn't such a case be very appropriate to purge Tuskegee of its 'undesirables'? I submit to you that such is the case. We are all threatened by this awesome power to dismiss any student for any or no reason. . . ." Even WSFA-TV admitted openly, in an editorial of April 10, that the administration's moves were designed "to weed out the troublemakers"—moves which it called drastic but necessary. As usual, "drastic" measures were considered necessary when used by the power structure but not when used by those fighting it.

The administration, of course, presented a different face to its friends. In a letter dated April 8 to Tuskegee alumni and supporters, President Foster wrote the following about "certain unfortunate developments":

> . . . The vast majority of students were opposed to these disruptive tactics and wished for reasonable solutions to the issues. Unfortunately, it is not easy to galvanize the many "quiet ones". . . .

This has been a difficult and unhappy experience for us all. We can only hope—and with some reason for optimism as we read the history of Tuskegee and of our society generally—that we shall all be stronger, wiser, and more dedicated in our efforts to enable Tuskegee to serve young people in the finest possible way. . . .

While pouring oil on the waters with one hand and pressuring the students into submission with another, the administration also moved directly and harshly against the so-called "determined, small core of trouble-makers." Criminal charges were filed against forty students, enjoining them against various actions, including "loitering or sitting in or around . . . Tuskegee Institute, committing any act calculated to disrupt the operation of Tuskegee Institute," etc. Trespassing notices were posted on all campus buildings for the period when the school was closed, and special trespassing letters were sent to twenty-four students. As for Michael Wright, he received extra-special treatment.

MICHAEL WRIGHT: That Sunday night, April 7, a lot of us split because we got the word that they were going to try and bust us. I went to Georgia with a few others and laid cool. Some of us went to St. Louis, some to the West Coast, and they'll never come back here.

On Monday, the school issued warrants for disturbing the peace against sixteen of us, including myself, with other charges pending. But we didn't know that at the time. We made phone calls to determine our status and as far as anyone could determine, there was no warrant out for my arrest. We did know there was an injunction against our being on campus. We went back there on Thursday, April 11. It was a beautiful place—no people to mess it up.

I asked the deputy sheriff if there was a warrant out for me. He said no, but that he wanted me to come down and talk to the Sheriff because he had an injunction to serve. I got in the car and went down to the jail. Sheriff Amerson was there and he pulled out the injunction. Then five minutes later, he smiled at me. I said, "Do you have a warrant for my arrest?" He smiled and said, "Yessuh." I just took that as best as you can.

Amerson was trying to set a $1000 bond on us—he wanted to keep us in jail. The people in the Establishment had told him to do so because if they could come up with more charges, they wanted us to be there—in jail. Amerson finally set it at $500 and I got out of jail on April 11.

On April 22, school reopened. Some ninety per cent of the students had filed readmission applications and over twenty-five hundred were readmitted fully clear while about ninety were admitted on probation. Fifty-four who had applied were not readmitted. Classes resumed with the injunction against "disruptive actions on campus" still in effect. Somehow, President Foster could reopen the school with a speech which concluded with these pompous, empty words:

> In the life of every individual and of every institution, there come times of great difficulty. It is during these periods . . . that those who are truly strong make themselves see clearly, think rationally, deal justly, and act courageously . . .

> As we leave this place today, may we join in mutual affection and in genuine commitment to our individual and institutional destinies.

There was one last battle still in progress. A complaint had been filed demanding reinstatement of the fifty-odd students who had applied for and been refused readmission. Support for them was mustered, including a legal defense fund headed by Ernest Stephens. On April 24, Judge Frank Johnson of the U.S. District Court for the Middle District ruled that the expulsion of those students had been unconstitutional and was thereby revoked. However—and it was a big however—this decision did not prohibit Tuskegee Institute from taking disciplinary action against them.

As could be predicted, the students were suspended that same day—with, of course, the right to hearings.

MICHAEL WRIGHT: From the hearings, eleven students (including myself) were put out of school again. They got rid of the people they wanted to get rid of, and that's pretty much the situation now.

Up until graduation, the atmosphere was one of extreme preoccupation on the administration's part about the possible burning of the school. They had armed guards all around the campus. Even the people out at the gate cutting grass had guns. Except for the four days when I was in Georgia, I spent all my time at Tuskegee and every time I stepped on the campus I got another charge against me. There are four of them now—I figure that they'll try to make one of them stick and I'll end up doing a maximum of six months. George Ware and Simuel Schutz also got arrested twice for trespassing. But the other brothers turned the jail out. All of them were armed. I think Amerson had grave reservations about shooting anyone.

We did about all we could, but people at Tuskegee really didn't have their shit together. There should have been more work—more honest, serious, courageous work. A lot of us were scared; we didn't know what to expect. Amerson was always talking about throwing all of us in jail for loitering. The students were terror-stricken. Some cats from South Carolina and Mississippi helped us, but after a while we all concurred that organizing was a bitch. We were trying to get money, to get things mimeographed, but the squeeze was on and it was difficult to even get a letter out. Another problem was that there had been no leaders in Unity. Our philosophy centered on being democratic. It would work out okay—we would elect a chairman at the current meeting for the next meeting. But after all the problems we ran into, I feel that there should have been some structure.

We sure learned about Amerson. Two years ago he got his support from people in Macon County. Students like Sammy Younge and myself were pushing for his election. Now the TCA and the Establishment are behind him. He's preoccupied with "order."

Michael Wright and the Tuskegee students of 1968 had experimented with seizing and holding power. They won concessions from the Tuskegee Establishment; they did not bow to the power of the visible whites on the Board of Trustees. The Tuskegee students of 1968 concentrated on making internal changes at their school, whereas Sammy Younge and his contemporaries of 1965 had worked to change the larger community. They were not unaware of the longstanding need for basic reforms at Tuskegee Institute, but the blatant segregation and white brutality forced their attention away from the campus itself. As voting restrictions eased and Jim Crow began to lose its force, as new concepts of black control and a measure of Black Power came to Tuskegee, it was inevitable that the students' attention would shift to their own home ground. Michael Wright then went about taking care of business in his time as Sammy Younge had done during his life.

The life and times of Sammy Younge, Jr., demonstrate that change, and the historical process must be seen from a long-range viewpoint. If one looks at, for example, the 1965 Montgomery demonstration or Sammy's work for the vote *in isolation*, one cannot perceive the significance of such actions. So it is with other events in the lives of all people. But the history of resistance to the most unique colonization experience known to mankind shows that the sixties must be recorded as an accelerating generation, a generation of black people determined that they will survive, a generation aware that resistance is the agenda for today and that *action* by people is necessary to quicken the steps of history.

Sammy Younge, Jr., understood this. He knew that those in power do not concede or relinquish their position without a fight, a skirmish, a struggle, a war in which violence and force will be used to keep the powerless oppressed. At the same time that those in power are napalming millions of people around the world and stock-piling massive piles of arms in their own country, they will say to the poor, to the colonized, to the blacks: love thine enemy, and violence is not the way.

As they kill babies of the Third World and proud black men such as Sammy Younge, they will try to keep the educational process an instrument of control, an instrument that teaches people to unconsciously accept their condition of servitude and pledge allegiance to the flag and serve the country on the high seas or as front-line troops in jungles far away from home.

Sammy Younge, Jr., served the United States well in the Navy.

He worked hard on a battleship blockading the Cuban coast, an act designed to protect white America.

He came home to Tuskegee, where George Wallace was the governor of Alabama.

He went with hundreds of other black students to the State Capitol in Montgomery to petition for the right to vote and to end police brutality in Selma and other parts of Alabama.

He worked in Macon County trying to register people to vote.

He went to the lily-white churches of Tuskegee and said: Open your doors, you hypocrites.

He picketed the banks and said: You have the power to change conditions.

He was known as a student leader, a nigger agitator.

A man who operated a Standard Oil gas station, an Alabama son of white America, killed him in cold black blood.

Index